What is Real?
My Search for Truth
In a World of Chaos and Confusion

ii

What is Real?
My Search for Truth
In a World of Chaos and Confusion
by Thomas M. Carter

Photo by SEAL SOC Mark T. Carter 2003

iv

This Book
is
Lovingly Dedicated
to
my children:

Brandon Reade

Jennifer Suzanne

Trevor Lincoln

Mark Thomas

Noel Christina

Shalynn

Taylor Michael

I gratefully acknowledge the loving support and common-sense suggestions of my wife, Cindy, and my dear sister, Susan.

Table of Contents

Preface

How do I Open my Soul to Knowledge and Truth?

It takes great courage to authentically ask oneself, "What is True?"

I have asked myself that question many times. If you are fervently seeking an answer to that question, if you are sincerely and passionately yearning and searching for truth, then this book is written for you.   Like myself, perhaps you have sought understanding and clarity in this chaotic and confusing world. Perhaps you are searching for answers from a place of puzzlement, perplexity, and confusion. I have been there. What I have learned about finding truth may also be an illuminator for you to shine the way forward through the dark thickets of bewilderment, illusion and deception, as you seek to find that "pearl of great price." For the person who is fettered with uncertainty and delusion, who seeks to find and know the truth of things but is not sure of where or how to find it, or even if it is possible to find, here are some ideas to consider. For the sincere and committed individual who is earnestly seeking peace and enlightenment, but whose soul may be clouded by fear or pain, or whose conscience has been seared by the abusive actions of others, but is still pressing forward doing the best he can, there is a brightness of hope that the truth will set you free.

We are all vulnerable to error and deception as part of our human nature, each having our share of petty rationalizations, diversions, and substitutes for truth. For those of us who at times are passive or just indifferent, here are some ideas on how to address these stumbling blocks. For the faint of heart who avoids the straight and narrow path of truth out of laziness or fear, or for the hardened heart who is clinging to his own prideful conception of truth, this book will challenge you. It will confront the cavalier followers of the shallow, conventional thinking of the day, or those who flee to shelter their own interest or bias at the first sign of controversy. It will hopefully engage one whose emotion or passions threaten to overcome his commitment to the truth. It will meet head-on those who have a closed mind and think that they already know everything that's important. I have been all of these people.

I am hoping that the earnest and genuine seeker of truth may here find clarity and a path forward. Even for the disillusioned or cynical, I hope he may find hope and courage to invest in and engage in the marvelous pursuit of truth. Most of all, this book is for him or her who is *willing to believe*, and then to *accept*, what is true.

The book is the story of my own lifelong search for truth, and of my own personal experience, as I have walked the gauntlet of the refining fire of life: the paths of perplexity, uncertainty, and, yes, the paths of temptation, denial, wrong behavior, repentance, and deep adversity. I have learned that as I seek the truth with real intent, with faith in the Author of all truth, with a willing, teachable and obedient heart, I become empowered to discern the truth, and hold on to it with confidence as my guide. *I love the truth.*

The truth is the most precious gift that I aspire to, the ultimate treasure. But it is bought with a corresponding price: that of a resolute search, a necessary sacrifice of one's preconceived notions and unworthy actions, the courage to willingly accept and embrace its reality, and the commitment and fortitude to act consistent with it.

I continue on that journey, with the certain faith and assurance that the truth will blossom in my soul until the Perfect Day, when I will be able to see all things as they really are.

I challenge each reader of this book to make the commitment to seek out, believe in, embrace, and defend the truth with all of your might. If you do this, you will find confidence in your understanding, and the joy and the "peace of God that passeth all understanding"[1], as you transcend the mortality of this world, and rise to view the riches of eternity, to where "eye hath not seen, nor ear heard, neither have entered into the heart of man, the things which God hath prepared for them that love him." (1 Corinthians 2:7)[2]

(Note for the reader)

Throughout the text, in the interest of common use and simplicity, the use of the masculine word "him," or "he," is meant also to refer to the feminine "her" or "she".

Introduction

I have always wanted to understand things, to know how the world works, and to have confidence in what is real, and what is true--a hunger for figuring things out. This stemmed from my earliest childhood—one of eleven children, and the son of a farmer/rancher in Wyoming and Montana.

As I grew up I loved the flowers and trees, the mountains and streams, and science projects. Early on, I knew I wanted to be a doctor, and this dream became my star. I wanted to know about everything. In response to my constant questioning. "Why" this? and "Why" that? My Dad frequently responded, "To make little boys ask questions!" My grandmother, who was a librarian, was always bringing the best books to our house, and I gained a great love for good books. Pets, home science projects, music lessons, growing up close to the earth--all of these elements--distilled into defining my personality with a desire to figure things out, to understand what is real, to gain knowledge, to know the truth about things.

My parents were politically conservative, and we grew up in a devoutly religious home, members of The Church of Jesus Christ of Latter-Day Saints. My Dad was known as the most honest man in town. I remember him telling me one summer evening while irrigating the pasture, "Tom, always be honest!" As I went to college and began exploring the public world, I was struck by how people think differently about religion, politics, and philosophy. I became engaged in the political issues and controversies of the time, and I understood and embraced conservative thinking. I think I did this at the time because that was what my parents thought, and I respected them, and it made sense to me. I carried this thinking clear through university and into medical school. I spent my last year of undergraduate university at George Washington University in Washington, DC, where I also got a job working with my home state (Wyoming) Senator, Senator Clifford Hansen. I worked as a legislative assistant on health-related matters and on national health insurance. During that time, I was exposed to the full spectrum of conservative and liberal political thinking as well as secular philosophy. I roomed with students that had much different backgrounds than I and was introduced into thinking and behaviors that were antithetical to the values I had grown up with. Intriguing to me was that I was able to associate with and make friends with these people who had very different values and philosophies than my own. We shared common human feelings and aspirations, and a yearning to know what is true. Some of my best friends had fundamental opposing views on moral standards, religious belief, and political leanings. I remember one of my best friends confiding in me, "I can't believe that one of my best friends (myself) likes Ronald Reagan!" And, I learned that I could stand up for my own values and standards without losing respect and friendship.

This was when I started delving seriously into the world of philosophy, politics, religion, and human behavior. I found in a little used-bookstore the Essays of Ralph Waldo Emerson, which was a revelation to me that instilled confidence in listening to my inner voice. I had already gained a conviction of my religious beliefs, and this provided a sure standard and path for my personal behavior, but this conviction did not necessarily extend into the multitude of other issues that I was confronted with, such as politics, social, and economic problems. Over the next few years, I seriously studied and considered other political and religious philosophies.

In the midst of all this, so often, I have asked myself, "What is true? What is real?" Why do good people with sincere intentions believe so differently? Why can't we agree with rational discussion on important issues? Are there right answers and wrong answers? If so, how can one find the right answers, and more importantly, how can we become united in a common understanding of what is true?

That is the genesis of this book. That is what has motivated me to seriously and comprehensively explore and examine my beliefs, and the foundations of what is true.

As I have done so, I have come to the conviction that it may indeed be possible to attain an understanding of truth, and that in the midst of all of our divergent personalities, outlooks, backgrounds, there is a common thread of humanity that can lead us to an understanding of the truth of things, and that can ultimately unite us as individuals in the human family.

Experience has taught me that intellectual and argumentative discussion about the endpoints of truth does not work in changing deeply held opinions and beliefs. It goes much deeper, to the well-springs of our humanity and to what motivates a person to think and to believe. It occurred to me that one must start with the basics, the foundations of knowledge and truth. And this is what I have attempted to do in the following pages.

A personal note

I do not claim to have any special access to what is true. I make no claim that I know everything or understand even the smallest portion of the infinite sphere of the totality of truth. And I am certainly subject to the petty weaknesses and distractions and prejudices common to people. Much of what I have learned has been learned the hard way, by the school of hard knocks, as I have at times been self-righteous and arrogant in my supposed higher virtue, and at other times been self-centered and a prey to the intoxications and vices of the mind and of the flesh. I have been in the dark places. *But I have learned that there is a way out of that*—through the enlightenment and power of truth--and that has imbued me with a passion for truth and is why I have written this book.

Hence, there are some things that I do know for sure, and these truths have led me on to others. As I have gained knowledge of a few things, I have learned somewhat of the process of finding what is true, and this knowledge is most precious to me, as I apply it to the many controversies and questions that I have faced, and that I face every day. It is a sublime, and powerful, experience of letting go of falsity and delusion, and then finding understanding of the world and seeing, at least in part, the way things really are.

And of finding power to rise to my better nature. This path towards knowledge of what is true is a sacred journey, and I am humbled, thrilled and grateful to know when I am on that path.

There is not a single answer to what is true (although I do believe that there do exist fundamental, absolute truths). The answer to what is true is not entirely what this book is about; the book is primarily about *embracing the question*--how to find truth. For each individual, this is a most personal and intimate challenge, for which he maintains sole responsibility and accountability. An understanding of what is true cannot be externally imposed upon a person. He must find it and accept it of his own free will. I have no interest in imposing my beliefs upon another; indeed, I recoil at the suggestion. My purpose is simply to share with gratitude those things which I have found to be true, and how I found them, hoping that this will help another to walk that straight and narrow path that leads to knowledge of things as they really are—the bright and shining star that is the secret hope of every man.

How to use this book

I have written this book in an ascending description of the importance of knowing truth, the difficulties involved in finding truth, to a description of what truth is, and then on to specific applications to pertinent issues of our time. Interspersed in the text are personal examples of how I, myself, have struggled and dealt with the problem of truth.

The interested reader may find it useful to explore the first few chapters, and then focus on the chapters he finds most pertinent to his own interest and life. Of course, the totality of truth encompasses every facet of existence, so the truths of each of these areas will build together to an understanding that all truth may be circumscribed into one magnificent whole. The principles of finding truth in one sphere of knowledge inevitably will apply to another sphere and on-and-on. I hope that what is written will be helpful to the reader in any aspect of his thinking where doubt and uncertainty arise.

1

My Search for Truth

Many years ago as a young High School student, I faced a situation that challenged my ability to find the Truth.

A charismatic high-school teacher seemed to connect to our group of vocational agriculture students, and we had lots of good learning and fun in class and with our extracurricular agriculture projects. He became a mentor of sorts and we looked up to him with awe and that youthful idealism of a promising friendship.

Mid-year, he began talking about how the school administrator hated him because he was doing such a great job with the students, and that he was a threat to the "powers that be" at the school. This was all cast in the framework of the "great teacher" being the target of envy and jealousy from those in authority. This played very well with us adolescent students already grappling with issues of authority.

Soon, he informed us that his teaching contract was not going to be renewed, and he wouldn't be coming back the next year. We took great umbrage at this and rallied around him. We believed his story, and were angry that our leader, friend, and hero was being thrown out unfairly. We sought an audience with the school administrator, but he was unwilling to even discuss the details with us. It seemed that he was impervious to our opinion. I was outraged and decided to take a public position of support for my teacher and friend. My father counseled me that perhaps I wasn't seeing the whole picture and to hold off until more information was available, but I would have none of it. I held onto my belief with such intensity that I was unwilling to see other viewpoints. I would not let go of it. I wanted to believe him. A friend and I circulated to the community a petition for his rehire. We drove house-to-house and claimed many signatures, and then presented the petition to the superintendent and the school board. It was summarily rejected without explanation. I was devastated and very angry.

In the ensuing days, I asked myself over and over "How could this be?" "What is the truth of this situation?" "Is he a good man, or not?" Where is the fairness here? I struggled to understand how different persons could view this "good" man so differently.

After the school year had ended, during the summer, information began trickling in of improper actions the teacher had been taking with some students. I began to remember certain questionable actions and comments that I had witnessed myself but had ignored or discounted. (I confess that I was naive and oblivious of what was going on. I had been taught by my parents not to drink and carouse late at night and in no way was a party-boy). When I shyly ventured to ask my teacher about the rumors that I had heard about him partying with students, he became defensive and evasive. He was relocating anyway, so it was easy for him to stop talking with me, and I was hurt as he withdrew, and our friendship faded. Gradually the façade that he was maintaining with me fell away and I began to see how it really was. The straw that broke the camel's back was when I learned that he had been supplying students with alcohol. Then, I could understand that issues of confidentiality in a pending investigation had prevented the superintendent from discussing the case with me, and that the teacher had been let go for inappropriate behavior with students. It all became quite clear.

I felt so foolish that I had been duped. But I was grateful that I could now see the situation clearly, and that brought confidence. I wrote letters to my friends. Some of them criticized me for not being loyal to the teacher. I met with the administrator and apologized for causing him so much trouble. I was very surprised that he was very kind with me and said that I hadn't actually caused him any trouble at all. He shook my hand with respect. Then, I was at peace with it, but with eyes wider open.

I learned some very important lessons from this experience: The truth isn't always what it appears to be. Sometimes it is hard to discover and may take time to become apparent. Until then, it's better to be humble and tentative before leaping to conclusions. We can discount the truth, or even ignore it, by what we passionately want, or do not want, to believe.

Some truths have come easily to me, but others have come after great effort and great turmoil and have even taken a lifetime to discover and clarify. As I have relied on simple truths and basic principles, I have come to learn, in cases of doubt, that it is more important to trust people that I know are wise, (if I had trusted my Dad, I would have been spared an embarrassing situation) than to understand right now the whole truth about everything. It's important to obey the commandments of God and do what you know is right, even if you don't understand it all. By so doing, in this instance, (by not participating in underage drinking), I was protected from the unsavory involvement of this man's actions. There is great safety in obedience, as we wait in faith for the whole picture to unfold.

Later in life, I experienced other controversies regarding what is true, and I still do. Indeed, the central issues of my life have always revolved about the question, "What is true?" As I have learned to accept, honor, and obey the simple truths of which I do have knowledge, I have experienced peace, confidence, and happiness, as I look forward with faith to the knowledge of greater things to come.

2

The Problem of Truth

How will it be

if nobody can say,

"I Know!"

We live in a time when the actual truth about so many things can be really hard to find. Every day each of us is confronted with circumstances that challenge our ability to find and discern truth. The world is in chaos and confusion over what is true. Consider your own personal conversations over what is important in your life, the challenges that you and your family face every day, the most salient moral issues of the day, the political and public discourse. As you think about it, you may realize that each of these issues revolves about the central question of our time: What is True?

In this age of unprecedented ease of communication and technological access to information, one would think that the truth of any particular subject or controversy would be easy to find. But we find distractions, distortions, rationalizations, false representations, and demagoguery that actually distract from or obscure the truth, often making knowledge more elusive than ever. Simple issues become complicated by the plethora of conflicting information and viewpoints disseminated to the masses in a near-instantaneous news cycle. Controversies are debated and argued by skillful "experts" until confusion reigns. I frequently ask my children what they think about a particular current controversy, and they often respond, "Dad, it's just too complicated and I'm confused!"

"Information overload" seems to almost overcome our ability to intelligently and rationally analyze the important issues of our time. Our world has confused information with knowledge. And although much knowledge is available in the information at our fingertips, we are left in frustration sifting through the sheer magnitude of details presented to us by the mass media. Often, rather than rationally and thoughtfully analyzing these important issues, we settle for the easy road, the conventional opinion, the herd mentality, hoping that "everybody else can't be wrong." We are tempted to join the "Worldly lifestyles (that) are cleverly reinforced by the rationalization, 'Everybody is doing it,' thus fanning or feigning a majority."[3] Or, we rely on so-called experts, the "talking heads" in the media to inform us of how we should perceive any particular issue. "Opinion polls" are used to reflect, and even influence, the popular opinion of the day. The conventional thinking, reduced to stereotypical and ideological camps, easily becomes our guide and we are tempted to fall in line with the popular thought rather than embarking on our own individual and independent course of determining truth.

An illusion of truth

We are also prone to fall into the false notion that, because of our access to so much information, we "know it all". In America today, everybody thinks they know everything. This is an *illusion* of knowing the truth. And it satisfies our feeling that we *should* know the answer. Everybody has his own opinion on just about every subject. But very few are interested to defend that opinion with rational discussion. It's as if merely having an opinion, or belief, is enough--equated with knowing the truth.

But we are actually quite insecure in our knowledge of truth, so we don't like to be challenged, and we are even more uncomfortable and reluctant to explain or defend what we believe. Sometimes we don't even know what we believe! We may have our opinion, and that's that! Increasingly it's becoming socially impolite to even discuss the things that people might disagree on, like politics or religion (the most important things). Like the Greeks of old in their rejection of Socrates and his prickly questions, we really don't like to be confronted with the inconvenient contradictions of our shallow conventional thinking. Could this be a sign that our culture is losing its perception of what is real, and what is true?

In such an atmosphere, is it any wonder that so many have become disillusioned, cynical, discouraged, and revert to prejudicial, shallow, self-absorbed, and narcissistic thinking? Many simply check out of the current debate, distracting themselves from the hard thinking with what money can buy, unrestrained social media, trendy entertainment, and so-called fun. Some participate in shallow, vapid, virtue-signaling politics which may make them feel good, but which accomplish little, and often degenerate towards a downward spiral of frustration, division, polarization, and even hatred. Some feel so confused that it seems impossible to engage in the popular discourse intelligently and rationally, so they may choose to ignore what is going on in the world with a vain hope that "everything will just work out all right." They may conclude that, "I have no power or influence to change things," or "What I think doesn't matter." Such cynicism breeds complacency, ignorance, malaise, and isolation, which paralyzes us in taking action. It erodes self-reliance, self-respect, responsibility, confidence-- the very foundations of freedom and liberty.

Or, for those who know the truth about a *few* things, some then assume that they know the truth about *all* things. In arrogance and pride from their blessed knowledge of a few key truths, such as the existence of God, or a particular philosophy, they thence harbor the vain notion that *all* of their opinions are true, without subjecting them to a rigorous test or standard. This false security can be a serious obstacle to knowledge of truth and may confine one's vision and ability to see things as they really are in some of the simplest, yet vital, issues of life. There is a danger that when one grasps untested, dogmatic opinions about little things, his commitment to the truth of more important issues may become compromised.

I believe that the greatest challenge that the world, and each of us as individuals, now face is the age-old question, "What is true?" This question is pervasive and ever-present in our lives every day. Asking the question, "What is true," is a strategy for clear-sightedness – for careful looking – for questioning – and for open-mindedness. How we answer that question will largely determine our ability to navigate and succeed in the challenges of our lives, and to fulfill the possibilities of our destiny. As we take seriously and honor this question, we embark on the road to reality, to seeing things as they really are. And this is why it is so important to discover our pathway towards truth. This is how we discover who we are and our own place in the world. And that knowledge will largely direct our actions, with the most profound consequences that lie therein.

How will it be, then, if we lose the ability to discover truth; how will it be when nobody will say, "I know?"

Our next chapter, "The Nature of Truth," takes on that challenge as we explore the foundations of knowledge, reality and truth.

3

The Nature of Truth

Two millennia ago, at his inquisition of Jesus Christ, Pontius Pilate posed the question, "What is truth?" (John 18:38) This question has reverberated through the centuries, and is still the most pertinent, penetrating, and essential question of our day.

These days, the world is so confused about what truth is that many even doubt its existence. The very concept of truth is under attack. Some imagine that everything is subjective or relative, that there is no tangible reality. We fancy that one person's "truth" is as valid as another's, that each person owns his "personal" truth, even if diverse opinions are self-contradictory and mutually exclusive.[4] We may have a vain idea that our own opinion should carry the same credence as that of any other, just because we choose to believe it. Not much has changed since 2500 years ago, when Protagoras exclaimed to Socrates, "What is true for you is true for you, and what is true for me is true for me."[5] This comes from a wrong-headed philosophy that truth is internally defined by each individual rather than externally established as the foundational law of the universe. By this deception, the intrinsic value of the individual becomes confused with his opinions.

This is a false and pernicious doctrine, because it prevents us from finding truth, and paralyzes us in distinguishing our own bias from the truth. It effectively destroys our ability to defend the truth. There is always a right and a wrong answer, or a "good, better, best" to every question. (Yes, sometimes there are equally right answers, but they cannot be self-contradictory.) There is right and wrong. Right is truth; wrong is falsehood. But if we can't, or won't, accept that fact, we won't be able to identify the "good, better, best" --the truth--much less choose to believe and act on what is true.

Truth is an absolute. It is sovereign, supreme, and stands above and alone as the ultimate and final arbiter and fact. Truth shines pervasively, independently, and transcends error and deception. It is not created but is self-existent. Although our perception of the truth may evolve with experience, what is true does not evolve from one moment to the next. We do not invent truth. Our imperative is to discover truth. The truth will not conform to us--we must conform to the truth. This can be a very daunting task! For the truth of things can be very complicated and multifaceted as one drills down to the essence of the question at hand.

Plato described truth as, "... knowing things as they really are." And modern revelation states, "Truth is the knowledge of things as they are, as they were, and as they are to become."[6] In other words, truth is reality, past, present, and future.

The Koran states, "We cast the truth against the falsehood, so that it demolishes it, and lo! it vanishes away...." (Qur'an 21:18)

In the Bible, truth is likened to a double-edged sword that divides light from darkness.[7] It is the great moderator. It is the great separator of good and evil. It is the ultimate certainty. The brightness of truth may illuminate our consciousness as a vision of hope and light which becomes our constant guiding star.

> "The fleeting glimpses that I have been able to have of truth can hardly convey an idea of the indescribable luster of truth, a million times more intense than that of the Sun we daily see with our eye. In fact, what I have caught is only the faintest glimmer of that mighty effulgence."[8] -- Mahatma Gandhi

The essence of truth for each person emanates from the spark of divinity within his soul--the reality of all of that which he is and which he possesses, and which he can become--his very identity—and his final destiny. To honor and nurture that spark is our great task and our great privilege.

Truth vs. Belief—a crucial distinction

While truth is a fundamental fact, or standard--the way things really are, an absolute--opinion or belief is not. Many people have opinions or beliefs that seem to work for them (their "truth") that may be taken on the basis of their personal experience. People may feel happy/sad/angry based on these opinions, even if there seems to be no rational basis for them (they may be based on incomplete information or simply the inherent limitations of humanity.) They often rapidly evolve into established beliefs, and beliefs are commonly misunderstood to be knowledge. Reasonable people may have differing experiences, opinions or beliefs on any given subject, but this should not be necessarily construed as truth. (We should always respect others' opinions or beliefs, even if they appear to stem from flawed thinking. Peoples' experiences are valid and need to be acknowledged. As we respectfully acknowledge these opinions and beliefs in a setting of respect and tolerance, we set the stage for rational conversation, and this can help people to let go of their flawed beliefs. Perhaps we may also find ourselves letting go of our flawed beliefs!)

So often, we prematurely cast our opinions and beliefs as truth, which may lead to dogmatic rigidity. Until one has tested his opinions and beliefs against a reliable standard, and is confident of their truth, the honest course is to represent them merely as "opinions," reserving flexibility to change them with additional information. This is why it is so important to inform and educate oneself broadly. It's right to have an opinion, and still be open to new information that may modify it. This is the path of honesty and integrity. As the Greeks learned long ago:

> "... do not have one mind, and one alone
> that only your opinion can be right.

> Whoever thinks that he alone is wise,
>
> his eloquence, his mind, above the rest,
>
> comes the unfolding, shows his emptiness.
>
> A man, though wise, should never be ashamed
>
> of learning more and must unbend his mind.
>
> "… it would be best if men were born
>
> perfect in wisdom, but that failing this
>
> (which often fails) it can be no dishonor
>
> to learn from others when they speak good sense."[9]
>
> --from Sophocles, "Antigone"

Should we be asking ourselves if our opinions and beliefs are true? This question leads us to the most fundamental challenge that each of us faces:

"Will I adjust my opinions and beliefs until I find the Truth?"

"Will I believe what is true?"

It is foolishness to believe that which is not true, and to be captive to one's bias or ignorance. Only a fool will hold onto false opinion in the light of truth. How pathetic it is to live our whole lives holding on to our prejudices and false notions! What a tragedy to discover in our mature years that we have been hostage all of our lives to false and corrupted traditions and beliefs and are headed to our graves having learned nothing!

> "Then Old Age and Experience, hand in hand,
>
> Lead him to death, and make him understand,
>
> After a search so painful and so long,
>
> That all his life he has been in the wrong."[10]
>
> -- Earl of Rochester

This brings to mind an image of a patient of mine who, in his old age, still clings to his belief that the Holocaust was a fiction promulgated by the Jews to perpetuate their victimhood. He had served as a young man as a personal secretary to Mussolini and claimed to know Hitler personally as well. He was a prominent diplomat in the Italian State Department. After the war, he emigrated to the United States, and now, as an old man, he has never given up the prejudices and wrong-headed beliefs of his earlier days. He is a bitter, close-minded, and lonely old man. Although this is an extreme example, how many people do you know that still cling to their prejudices, false notions, and debunked stories that perpetuate their victimhood and excuses for failure?

Nevertheless, we must be very cautious about claiming that we know the truth. "For now, we see through a glass, darkly..."[11] (1 Corinthians 13:12).

A well-known poem, "Blind Men and the Elephant"[12] (see appendix) illustrates how easy it is to see only a part of reality, depending on our vantage point. Each man, observing an elephant from a different vantage point, describes what he indeed narrowly observes, but is an incomplete picture of the whole. It would be impossible for each of these men to know the whole truth of the elephant from his own restricted viewpoint. How often do we jump to conclusions of reality and truth from a preliminary or incomplete knowledge of the facts, or from a limited perspective?

Although we may believe that our opinion about a particular subject is true, we would do well to carefully consider the reasons we believe as we do, inform ourselves of other viewpoints, and test our opinion or belief against a durable standard.

This starts with identifying what our beliefs are. (See table 1) Then we can analyze them, compare them to other extant opinions, and test them.

<u>Table 1</u>: What Do I Believe?

- What are the major social, political, religious controversies of the day?

- What issues are important to me and my loved ones now?

- What are the various opinions and beliefs on these controversies?

- What are my opinions and beliefs on these controversies?

- Why do I hold certain opinions or beliefs on each of these?

- Where do I go for knowledge of the truth about these issues and controversies?

- Is it important to me to know the truth about these issues? If so, why?

- What am I willing to do to find the truth about these things?

- How will my life be affected by knowledge of the truth of these things?

4

Believe What is True

"... the human understanding is so imbued with feeling and tinctured with the will and its passions that it is inclined to believe what it prefers."[13] -- Francis Bacon

Why do people choose to believe as they do?

People generally believe what they want to believe.

This "want to believe" is very powerful. It stems from various motives that are common to us all.

Of course, most of us want to believe the truth. We all start there. But, somewhere along the way, we become vulnerable to other motives. It takes effort and focus to distinguish our motives that will actually lead to knowledge of truth from those that will cloud our understanding of what is real.

Tradition--It is natural and comfortable to believe according to the traditions and culture that we have grown up with or that which was taught by our parents. This is a powerful determinant of belief. It can be a blessing if we grow up with true traditions, or a curse if we are taught according to false and corrupted traditions. A great example of this is religion. Most people in the world hold to the religion that they were exposed to in their youth. How many times do you hear, "I was raised a _____ and I will always be a _____"? It is easy to follow the religious traditions of our parents, especially in such a personal and pervasive way of thinking. Indeed, this tradition shapes our very identity, so it becomes our frame of reference from which we view the world, our comfort place, and our inherent bias.   Another common belief directed by tradition is the political preference we hold. "Conservative" vs "liberal" is a common world view that is easily adopted according to the traditions we have learned in our home environment. (The issue here is not whether a particular religion or political philosophy is false or corrupt, but whether it is accepted based on tradition, rather than independent search, testing, and confirmation.)

Ignorance --"Ignorance is bliss" goes the saying, and so it may seem to those who will not lend the time and energy to be informed. Ignorance relieves of us of a huge load of care. Whether from a lack of education, of being informed about the world around us, a lack of interest, or of a purposeful "studied ignorance," it is a powerful excuse for not seeking truth. Indeed, it allows one to blithely float in the controversies of our time without even having an opinion or belief. It has been said that, "Truth to some people is when thoughts appear in their head and they believe them". One can then simply believe what he wants to believe, even if he doesn't even know why he believes. This goes hand-in-hand with simple laziness. So, some people are confused in their beliefs simply because they have not made the effort to become informed. They are too lazy to seek out the truth, and thus take the easy road to believe what is most convenient.

Yes, the world is vast; we can't know the truth about everything. So, we need to decide *what the important questions are*, what interests us the most, and is relevant to our lives—that which will govern our beliefs and thence our actions: like bringing up our children well, reducing suffering in the world, voting right, saying the right thing in conversation, serving where needed, etc. These actions will be governed by our beliefs and enhanced by our knowledge of how the world really is.

Information and facts provide the foundation for rational and enlightened thought and discussion. Although many do not know not where to find the truth, or have not been exposed to a fair hearing of it, in this era of information, it really lies at our fingertips (i.e. the internet), and only takes a commitment of time to search it out. This also underscores the imperative for those who know truth to share it with others.

Self-interest—Peoples' desires or fears for themselves—their legitimate or illegitimate self-interest--may lead them to choose to believe whatever serves their purpose or conforms to their personal lifestyle, interest, agenda, preferred behavior, or monetary advantage. A good example of this is when we vote for the political party that promises us the best handout. When our interest is at stake, it's most easy to believe what bolsters and confirms that interest. You see this in the convoluted and ritualistic rationalizations of one who is defending his destructive lifestyle—whether it be an addiction, or one outside the commonly accepted norms, values and principles, i.e. one who is breaking the law or sustaining a lifestyle which he knows is wrong. Even when our self-interest is legitimate, we tend to choose to believe that which bolsters and confirms it. As Goethe well said, "As are the inclinations, so are the opinions."

Emotion—Our emotional response to any particular issue may be intense and overwhelming, and actually generate a "need to believe" that drives us to incredible lengths. Sometimes this takes the form of "wishful thinking" as we desperately attempt to create a reality that soothes our emotions. I experience this frequently when trying to discipline my children with "tough love." I would so much want to believe the best of them, even when they are misbehaving. And, it hurts me to discipline them when I love them so much. We may also generate emotion to comfort an abused conscience. Sometimes our emotion can be so strong that it overpowers any constraints of truth. Fear is a powerful motivator and is often connected to our very sense of safety and identity. Pain, physical or mental, inflicted accidentally, or by the abusive actions of others may direct our belief to what seems to be a safe haven. A good example of this is the pervasive distrust and altered view of authority that comes to one who has been abused, physically or emotionally, as a child. Or of the devastating emotional baggage that one carries who has been sexually abused. This takes many forms, such as denial,

("denial is a wonderful thing!"), rationalization to meet our own preferred lifestyle, needs or wants, and even illusion--the illusion of truth: the plethora of information and the ease of communication in our world can easily "stack the deck" with an excess of information, sometimes false information, or unverified information, creating false confidence and an illusion of knowledge.

As we let our emotions dominate our opinions and beliefs, we gradually close off our awareness of what is really true. This may become almost an unconscious act if we are not careful to test our emotions against reliable standards of truth. As we consciously deny the truth, we betray our most authentic identity, and corrupt our souls. We are then vulnerable to outright deception by the insidious sophistries and lies promoted by those seeking power, money, or the honors of men.

Addictions overwhelm one's natural ability to perceive truth, and are always associated with a distorted or perverted narrative of what is true. Layers upon layers of twisted thinking perpetuate the unrealistic thought patterns of the addict, whether his addiction is to drugs, sex, gambling, or any other addictive behavior. That is why addictions are so destructive.

Pride—a powerful force that inhibits our commitment to truth when we magnify our own genius, or don't want to admit that we were wrong. The need to be right or to win at all cost, even that of our own integrity, is a stunning betrayal of our authentic self. Here is a personal example of how pride can get in the way of seeing things as they really are:

I was at the nursery buying plants for my garden. I found an interesting plant with the tag "Mexican Heather, $3.99." I took the plant, along with my other purchases, to the counter to pay. The clerk said, "No, that is not the right tag. That plant sells for $7.99." I argued, "Well, it was marked $3.99, and I expect to pay that amount." We argued and I dug in my heels, insisting to pay what the plant was marked. He insisted that the plant was marked by mistake (the tag was actually just lying haphazardly on the tray). It got rather heated, and finally, the clerk just gave in and said he wouldn't charge me anything for the plant. So, victoriously I paid for the other plants and went to my car. I had a sheepish feeling that perhaps I had been rude. "No, I was right." But, "maybe you were a jerk about it." Then, I realized that my pride had got in the way of me treating the clerk fairly. I had supposed that he was being dishonest, but he was really just trying to do the right thing. Pride had prevented me from seeing the truth of the situation. I finally just went back in and apologized to the clerk. It just turned things around and made everybody happy. He was so kind to me and I could tell he appreciated my apology. Ironically, the admission of my mistake felt like a huge victory.

Pride of ownership of a particular opinion or belief often leads to what has been called "moral narcissism", described by Roger Simon in his book, *I Know Best*. "What you believe, or claim to believe or say you believe—not what you do or how you act or what the results of your actions may be—defines you as a person and makes you 'good...' You are what you proclaim your values to be, irrespective of their consequences. That is moral narcissism."[14]   We see this in the obnoxious "virtue signaling" from those crying "racism," "bigotry," when their own private actions do not conform to their preaching. In other words, "actions speak louder than words."

Another form of pride is "the corrupted intent that comes from those with seared consciences who willfully offend the truth to protect evil motivations and wrongful actions. They clutch their biases hysterically and blindly regardless of whom they destroy. This is a counterfeit for seeking and standing on truth. To seek truth requires them to clean up their act, which would require them to be responsible for the consequences of their actions and beliefs and words." --Susan Carter

Disobedience to the laws of the universe and of God is a form of pride and clouds our mind and corrupts our intent to seek the truth.[15]

Herd mentality --"Everybody else believes it." The conventional thinking offers a powerful excuse to save us from the work of seeking our own path to truth.

Bias—We all have biases that are a compelling motivation to our belief. Our biases are often so deeply instilled into our sub-consciousness that we may not even be aware of them. They control our vantage and initial response to any question. They are the "colored glasses" through which we see the world. When combined with misplaced pride and the compulsion to always be right, our biases indeed become powerful motivators to believe what we want to believe. Sometimes we hold onto our biases almost as a blanket of security, and to give them up seems to threaten our very sense of safety and identity. Indeed, it is difficult even to be aware of and to identify our biases. They seem to come naturally. As Justice Anthony Kennedy has stated, "Bias is easy to attribute to others and difficult to discern in oneself."[16] Of course, our biases and our assumptions will be colored by our experiences and our personal beliefs, but when we accept the misconception that we are unable to change our biases, this can paralyze our efforts to see the truth clearly. It is true that our biases *seem* inherent and inevitable, but it's not as if we have *no power* over them. As intelligent and purposeful human beings, we can generate insight to identify and inform our biases and develop the will and power to give them up, if necessary, in favor of the truth. I truly believe this. (See chapter 15, "Truth and Bias."}

———————————

People usually hold on to their opinions or beliefs passionately, but this does not make them true. The human mind has a powerful, amazing and incredible ability to believe what it wants. Often, we succumb to a "need to believe" that overpowers any semblance of sane thinking as we are confronted by fears, superstitions, prejudices and imagined slights, fantastic and ridiculous tales that have no connection with reality.

As illustration, consider what Thomas Carlyle writes in his classic work, *On Heroes, Hero-Worship, and the Heroic in History*, as he discusses the antiquated beliefs of paganism:

"Surely it seems a very strange-looking thing this Paganism; almost inconceivable to us in these days. A bewildering, inextricable jungle of delusions, confusions, falsehoods and absurdities, covering the whole field of Life! A thing which fills us with astonishment, almost, if it were possible, with incredulity, -- for truly it is not easy to understand that sane men should have worshipped their poor fellow-man as a God, and not him only, but stocks and stones, and all manner of animate and inanimate objects; and fashioned for themselves such a distracted chaos of hallucinations by way of Theory of the Universe: all this looks like an incredible fable. Nevertheless, it is a clear fact that they did it. Such hideous inextricable jungle of misworships, misbeliefs, men, made as we are, did actually hold by, and live at home in. This is strange. Yes, we may pause in sorrow and silence over the depths of darkness that are in man; if we rejoice in the heights of purer vision he has attained to. Such things were and are in man; in us too."[17]

"We shall begin to have a chance of understanding Paganism when we first admit that to its followers it was, at one time, earnestly true. Let us consider it very certain that men did believe in Paganism; men with open eyes, sound senses, men made altogether like ourselves; that we, had we been there, should have believed in it..."[18]

These primitive people, like us, certainly had access to truth; but the point is that they, like us, have missed the truth at some very crucial points.

Yes, let us recognize that man is still subject to error and deception. In our own day, absurd and fantastic beliefs abound still as ever before. As we look carefully at the conventional wisdom of our time and the beliefs extant in the world today, we may recognize some absurdities and falsities that still plague the human race. Perhaps they are more subtle and less unbelievable (to us) than previously. Perhaps they are more deceptive and insidious now because they contain more elements of truth. As we consider our own vulnerability to fraud and deception, is it possible that we might distinguish some of those absurdities in our own thinking? This leads us to a very important realization: *Let us be honest with ourselves: each of us is fallible.*

This leads to another crucial imperative:

Every man and woman has a solemn responsibility and duty to carefully examine his/her beliefs and the reasons why he/she wants to believe and chooses to believe as he/she does.

As he does that, he will discover that *he has power over what he believes.* This may be a novel idea to some, but it is a crucial insight that will lead him forward on the path of understanding things as they really are.

Whatever he believes, for whatever reason, a man's belief is his choice. Man has agency to choose his beliefs, and it follows that he is accountable for what he believes.[19]

Believe what is true

As we realize that our belief is really our own choice, we empower ourselves to actively choose what we will believe. *We may choose to believe that which is true.* My dear sister, Susan, gave me this challenge: "It will invite careful soul searching to find what price you are willing to pay or not to pay for the truth."

The ability to critically look at one's opinions and beliefs is a daunting task, but once honestly engaged in, can develop into a habit of choosing to believe what is true. The habit of constantly evaluating what is the actual truth of the controversies swirling about us is an exercise that will keep us alert and always vigilant. This may seem overwhelming at times, but it starts with our commitment to believe the most fundamental truths of our lives, and often these most fundamental truths are the most difficult to look at.

Let's start with the most fundamental truth of all: that God exists, and that He is our Heavenly Father, and we are his children, created in his image. As we accept the reality of this truth, we can then apply this truth as a bedrock to the understanding of all other knowledge. This truth is the gateway, as it were, to all other truth. For those who do not believe in God, or do not want to believe in God, this is an invitation to explore and test this reality. (See more in chapter 12, "Truth and Religion.")

With a determination and commitment to believe what is true, the wise man will give up any false or corrupted motive that leads him to untruth. This is the path of integrity. He must be willing to give up his pre-conceived notions, prejudices, self-interest, and any particular or personal biases, even his lifestyle if necessary. He must put aside his emotions and feelings that may be distracting him from clearly viewing the truth. He must become intelligently informed. He must be fearless, and courageous, and willing to pay any price for knowledge of the truth. As Ralph Waldo Emerson stated,

> "God offers to every mind its choice between truth and repose. Take which you please – you can never have both. Between these, as a pendulum, man oscillates. He in whom the love of repose predominates will accept the first creed, the first philosophy, the first political party he meets – most likely his father's. He gets rest, commodity and reputation; but he shuts the door of truth. He in whom the love of truth predominates will… abstain from dogmatism, and recognize all the opposite negations between which, as walls, his being is swung. He submits to the inconvenience of suspense and imperfect opinion, but he is a candidate for truth, as the other is not, and respects the highest law of his being." [20]

The benefit of believing what is true expands one's knowledge of reality and gives him power to successfully navigate the challenges of life, because he sees things as they really are, and is not deceived into false notions. Freed from false notions, he is able to act consistent with reality. True beliefs determine his correct actions, and his actions when consistent with reality and truth become powerfully effective in preserving and expanding his relationships, his success, and his ability to deal with whatever circumstances of life that befall him. In short, he overcomes his world: he transcends the petty circumstances of life and becomes master instead of slave.

To possess the truth, we must want to believe what is true, seek out what is true, and then make a choice to believe what is true.

To believe the truth is the supreme challenge for each person.

A mark of true manhood or womanhood is one's commitment to seek out, choose to believe, and embrace the truth.

With a firm commitment to believe what is true, we now turn to standards for truth that will lead us to recognize what is true and give us confidence as we step forward on to that exacting and rigorous path.

5

The Standard for Truth

Indeed, as we understand that truth is not created by our own effort and genius, but must be sought out as a precious jewel, a priceless possession, we are in a healthier place to find it. But this requires that we be an open, unfettered receptacle. We must be willing to believe.

As we are willing to accept the truth, we need landmarks and signposts to recognize and have confidence in our perception of it. We need something to hold on to, so when the winds of illusion and delusion, deceit and ignorance, beat against us, we may hold fast to the "iron rod" of truth and move forward with confidence and commitment.

Reliable standards for truth:

The discovery of truth is a process that involves three facets:

1. The truth will always be consistent with the facts.

Our generation is the beneficiary of the accumulated factual knowledge gained by humanity over the past several thousand years. We live in the age of information, of facts at our fingertips. Never before have so many facts and so much knowledge been available to so many. Coupled with that is freedom of expression in the free world of our time. Facts and freedom of thought and expression are the vital, necessary bases to rational thought and discussion.

"There's a great incendiary power in facts... In this age of fingertip internet searches, the ability to checkout facts gives one great power that allows him to call in question, or verify, whole narratives."[21] To do this, of course, one must be educated and informed. But with facts at his disposal, and the ability to call them into the argument, one can create a basis for disciplined, enlightened and rational discussion. Facts are as tethers to reality, and to truth. As John Quincy Adams famously stated, "Facts are stubborn things; and whatever may be our wishes, our inclinations, or the dictates of our passions, they cannot alter the state of facts and evidence"

In many cases, however, bare facts are not enough. Because we are not all scholars or historians, and even when we are informed, we may not know all of the facts. Indeed, the facts are not always knowable, or they may be incomplete or misrepresented. Facts usually need context to be understood accurately. "Wrong opinions and practices gradually yield to fact and argument: but facts and arguments, to produce any effect on the mind, must be brought before it. Very few facts are able to tell their own story without context to bring out their meaning."[22] –John Stuart Mill

People tend to cherry-pick the facts they want to support their position. Sometimes, even as we are presented with facts, we color them with attempts to interpret or modify them to our own ends. "We don't see things as they are; we see them as we are." (--Anais Nin)

A recent candidate for national political office stated, "We accept truth over facts,"[23] a perfect example of how facts can be suborned to one's own partisan narratives. When one puts his own conception of the truth ahead of facts, he is in trouble. Therefore, the use of facts requires judgment, honesty, and integrity. When advocacy uses or omits selective details, facts, and context, it denies persons a set of generally accepted facts to debate.[24] Without transparency and honesty, and an open mind, a rational debate becomes impossible.

Although we benefit from the expansive repository of information through modern information technology, is it possible that we place too much confidence in what information alone can tell us? Is it possible that we confuse information for reality? Is it possible that the true knowledge of who we are, where we came from, our destiny, and the answers to the perennial behavioral and social problems facing the human race, cannot be definitively found only in the physical facts of our temporal world? Does our reliance on our vast information technology distract and hinder us from the most important knowledge, the spiritual knowledge, that is vital in solving the behavioral, social, and spiritual problems that are threatening the very survival of the human race?

Sometimes, we may be so confused, conflicted, or compromised that we may not be able to intelligently analyze the facts, or we are unable or unwilling to listen to our conscience and make a decision. Our emotions may be so intense, and our need to believe so great, that we are unlikely to objectively look at the facts. We may be inexperienced or immature in our judgment of truth. This was my story as an immature high-school student (see Chapter 1, "My Search for Truth). In that case, I have found that it is helpful to listen to a trusted voice, or a reliable authority, even the commandments of God. This is when the voice of experience and wisdom may be so critical. Then, when the facts are clarified and our conscience is cleared, our judgment restored, we can find our way forward on the path of truth. This has saved many a person from error and deception. There is great safety in obedience to trusted sources.

2. Truth will always be based upon and consistent with fundamental, time-tested principles and moral values.

"I teach them correct principles, and they govern themselves." --Joseph Smith

Sound principles are "...the prejudices and traditions which millennia of human experience with divine means and judgments have implanted in the mind of the species."[25] "... One should guide his life by true principles... " (Lucretius, De Rerum Natura). True and sound values and principles are those that have been tried and tested in the forges of human experience. Here is one: The lesson of the ages is that virtue triumphs in the long run. In the broad arc of human history, virtue remains the standard for human behavior, and while deception and iniquity sometimes seem to dominate in the short term, history invariably admires and honors the virtuous man, and castigates and rejects the reprobate. This is a principle that has been proven and can be relied on. Other principles such as the fundamental worth of each human being, self-reliance and equality of opportunity, and moral values such as compassion and honesty are time-tested and universally applicable to the human experience. (See figures 2 and 3) In times of confusion and doubt, these values and principles provide a foundation and bulwark against the winds of deception and illusion, and may act as a lighthouse to guide through the waters of turmoil and the mists of the unknown. Sound principles can be relied upon even when the path forward seems murky and confusing, and sometimes are the only thing we can hold on to. "Important principles may and must be inflexible." (Abraham Lincoln in his last public address).

Often, we don't think about the values and principles which guide our belief and behavior. It is important that we identify those values and principles and prioritize them. As we do this, we may differentiate the superficial and trite from the deep and fundamental. It will enable us to balance and judge among seeming competing and conflicting values and principles. That will give us a basis and starting point in our quest for what is true.

These days, when even traditional fundamental values and principles are coming under attack, to sustain this onslaught we need to be grounded, informed, and clearly aware of what values and principles we rely on.

<u>Table 2</u>:

Examples of time-tested values

Love

Respect for others

Tolerance

Thrift

Patience

Hope

Honesty

Diligence

Compassion

Kindness

Loyalty

Friendship

Courage

Integrity

Trustworthiness

Generosity

Forgiveness

Humility

Selflessness

<u>Table</u> 3:

Examples of tried and true, sound principles

We are children of God, created in His image, with an inherent value
> as individuals, endowed with moral agency to
> choose our actions

"Do unto others as you would have them do unto you"

Respect for other people's rights and dignity

Free agency primarily to act and not be acted upon

Responsibility and accountability for one's actions

Rule of law—no one is above the law

All people are treated equally under the law

Individual freedom to pursue life, liberty, and happiness

Men should be equal in terms of opportunity to pursue happiness

The fundamental worth of each human being

Necessity for compromise

Obedience to God

The Ten Commandments

"Whatsoever a man sows, that shall he also reap"

Service to others

3. Truth will always be consistent with God-given revelation. This is the ultimate source of truth and the most reliable standard for truth.

Revelation may be described as the voice of God to man. It comes in many forms:

a. Overt revelation from God to man through his prophets and scriptures (such as the Bible and the Ten Commandments);

b. The enlightenment of our minds and the expansion of our understanding by the Spirit of God[26], which can also be described as the "ring of truth." This may come as new ideas or insights, sudden flashes of intelligence which we recognize as coming spontaneously from an external and divine source.

A great example of this is alluded to by Goethe: "... so-called awakenings, conversions... the becoming conscious of a great maxim, which is always an operation of the mind akin to genius. We arrive at it by insight, neither by reflection, nor by teaching, nor by tradition. Here it is the perception of the moral power which is anchored in faith, and so in the midst of the waves will feel itself in proud security. Such an apercu affords the discoverer the greatest joy, because, in an original manner, it points him to the Infinite; it requires no length of time for conviction; it leaps forth whole and perfect in a moment..."[27]

c. The incomparable and powerful voice of Nature (see chapter 11, "Nature and truth") I always feel enlightened and inspired when experiencing Nature.

d. The "still, small voice" in our hearts, which is indeed a revelation from God. This is a spiritual communication that is a common human experience, but not always recognized, and easily discounted, as it may be subtle, discerned by our mind and soul rather than our physical senses. "... behold, I will tell you in your mind and in your heart, by the Holy Ghost..."[28]

I have myself experienced this still, small voice, and have learned to recognize it as coming from a divine source, and to trust it. (See Chapter 20, "My Discovery of Truth") It only comes when my mind is open to it, seeking greater light and knowledge, and being willing to accept it. In this setting, it may come with an element of surprise, unrelated to thought patterns at the time, and always distinguishable as something external to my own thinking and consciousness. Sometimes it comes as a result of earnest seeking and questioning about a specific issue. Sometimes it comes as a wave of comfort, clarity, and enlightenment. It is always clear, subtle, yet convincing and surely uplifting, edifying, and "inspiring." It comes not through eyes and ears, but as a feeling, different than the usual physical emotions. It has invariably proven to be reliable.

This revelation of truth occurred to Aleksandr Solzhenitsyn in the despair and isolation of a Soviet prison. He relates his experience:

> "The guard was walking on tiptoe and kept signaling me not to make any noise as he led me down a corridor silent as the grave, through the fourth floor of the Lubyanka, past the desk of the section supervisor, past the shiny numbers on the cells and the olive-colored covers of the peepholes, and unlocked Cell 67. I entered and he locket it behind me immediately....
>
> "... by the time I arrived, the inhabitants of Cell 67 were already asleep on their metal cots...
>
> "At the sound of the door opening, all three started and raised their heads for an instant.... at this point the duty jailer brought in my cot, and I had to set it up without making any noise. I was helped by a young fellow my own age, also a military man. His tunic and aviator's cap hung on his cot. He had asked me, even before the old man spoke, not for news of the war but for tobacco. But although I felt openhearted toward my new friends, and although not many words had been exchanged in the few minutes since I joined them, I sensed something alien in this front-line soldier who was my contemporary, and, as far as he was concerned, I clammed up immediately and forever.
>
> "(I had not yet even heard the word 'nasedka' – 'stool pigeon' – nor learned that there had to be one such 'stool pigeon' in each cell. And I had not yet had time to think things over and conclude that I did not like this fellow, Georgi Kramarenko. But a spiritual relay, a sensor relay, had clicked inside me, and it had closed him off from me for good and all. I would not bother to recall this event if it had been the only one of its kind. But soon, with astonishment, and alarm, I became aware of the work of this internal sensor relay as a

constant, inborn trait. The years passed and I lay on the same bunks, marched in the same formations, and worked in the same work brigades with hundreds of others. And always that secret sensor relay, for whose creation I deserved not the least bit of credit, worked even before I remembered it was there, worked at the first sight of a human face and eyes, at the first sound of a voice— so that I opened my heart to that person either fully or just the width of a crack, or else shut myself off from him completely. This was so consistently unfailing that all the efforts of the State Security officers to employ stool pigeons began to seem to me as insignificant as being pestered by gnats: after all, a person who has undertaken to be a traitor always betrays the fact in his face and in his voice, and even though some were more skilled in pretense, there was always something fishy about them. On the other hand, the sensor relay helped me distinguish those to whom I could from the very beginning of our acquaintance completely disclose my most precious depths and secrets—secrets for which heads roll. Thus, it was that I got through eight years of imprisonment, three years of exile, and another six years of underground authorship, which were in no wise less dangerous. During all those seventeen years I recklessly revealed myself to dozens of people—and didn't make a misstep even once. (I have never read about this trait anywhere... It seems to me that such spiritual sensors exist in many of us, but because we live in too technological and rational an age, we neglect this miracle and don't allow it to develop.)"[29]

I quote this lengthy passage from *The Gulag Archipelago* to emphasize the reality and reliability of this "still, small voice" to which we are all entitled if we will listen for it, accept it, and honor it. Certainly, this revelation is available to all, but faith is required to accept it and act upon it.[30] It is the most sure and reliable guide to truth.

Even the ancients received these revelations. "Both Plato and Aristotle 'placed inspiration above reason and moral insight... because it comes from God' – for while reason is far from infallible, 'the sureness of inspiration, on the other hand, is like lightning.'"[31]

The ancient civilizations had a revelatory tradition that imbued their fundamental beliefs and culture. Ancient History scholar and historian, Hugh Nibley, explains that the ancient historian, Eusebius, "...develops the theory that all that is good and desirable in any civilization is actually a survival from some previous age of enlightenment when the Gospel was on the earth and men received light from heaven."[32] "... the common denominator of all ancient civilization which has been consistently overlooked, namely the image that each great civilization thought of itself as having been carefully planned in the beginning, all its rites and patterns handed down from above, a complete, perfect structure, planned in detail from the beginning as the faithful reflection of a heavenly prototype..."[33] The Greeks knew that revelation is the source of truth. This is the Platonic tradition, explained by Socrates: "This duty I have accepted, as I said, in obedience to God's commands given in oracles and dreams and in every way that any other divine dispensation has ever impressed a duty upon man."[34] He knew that without revealed truth, they were at best observing phantoms, shadows and effects, poor substitutes for the clarity of pure knowledge.[35] These revelatory traditions were corrupted and have been largely lost in the mists of time, with the notable exception of the Jewish revelations, recorded in The Holy Bible, and even these have been edited or changed so the original full meaning has been lost in some instances, and some translations of ancient revelations by Joseph Smith found in *The Pearl of Great Price*. But there is no doubt that they sprang from a common source. Many of the great minds have sought for the divine revelations that they realized were the key to knowledge of the truth. Hugh Nibley further explains: "So, what hope have we for real knowledge? Revelation, say Heraclitus: 'A man should listen to the spirits (daimones, the same word used by Socrates) as a child to an adult'; our individual minds are pretty dull, but through the ages there exists an unmistakable consensus of humanity about things, an ethos which is not the product of reason but of revelation.' There is a common divine logos in which we all have a share, and that is the one thing we can be really sure of, 'the one criterion of truth.'"[36]

The revelation of the "still, small voice" is different than the deep-seated bias, or "gut instinct" that we naturally grasp and hold on to in any controversy, and that we may confuse with the revelation of truth to our souls. As we learn to distinguish and separate our bias and emotion from this enlightenment, we find access to the pure, sweet voice of truth. It is an exciting dimension that challenges the core of our commitment to the truth. It opens a world of insight, understanding, and knowledge, as we learn to discern truths that we perhaps otherwise would never have imagined, and, that ultimately give us power to comprehend and change the world.

Men have always been dependent on revelation for knowledge that can't be gained by mortal observation. When they have discounted or rejected that revelation, they have been led into the most fantastic and crazy traditions and beliefs, which are regularly discredited and debunked as the following generations discover that they don't work. Thus, civilizations have risen and fallen as their uninspired traditions and philosophies have become corrupted, futile, and found to be vain and useless.

For many, the concept of direct revelation may seem a distant and improbable possibility, one that they have perhaps never considered or even thought of. "Who is God, that will descend to speak to me?" Or, perhaps, more easy to believe, is that God speaks to men only in a vague enlightenment of their minds, but certainly not in any specific or personal way. He certainly enlightens our minds and understandings, but the promise is also of something much more personal, and specific, and crucial to the discovery of truth.

To those who do not have a tradition or knowledge of the revelations of God, this is an invitation to search diligently and seek the revelation of His reality. Surely, God hears sincere supplication. It has always been so, for good men and women of all ages and nationalities have always been inspired with light and knowledge appropriate for them. Thus, we see inspired lives like Albert Schweitzer, Mahatma Gandhi, C.S. Lewis, and thousands, even millions of individuals, carrying their life burdens with faith, integrity, and endurance. They all have received revelatory light as a guide to their own walk from a loving God who has never abandoned the sincere searcher of truth. Mr. Gandhi referenced this when he noted that,

> "Truth is within ourselves. There is an inmost center in us all, where truth abides in fullness. Every wrongdoer knows within himself that he is doing wrong, for untruth cannot be mistaken for truth. Truth and righteousness must forever remain the law in God's world." [37]

For those who don't want to believe in God, or willfully deny the existence of God, and the reality of revelation from God to man, they cut themselves off from the very source of truth and light, and are left to flounder in a morass of ignorance, doubt, darkness, and the instability of their intellect and the futility of their own pride. As a man hardens his heart, blinds his eyes, deafens his hearing, turning backward and inward to his selfish, uninspired and corrupted motives, he betrays the very essence of who he is.

To every person in his daily walk, and in his moment of extremity and great need, is given the light to move forward on the path of truth, if he will accept and embrace that light and revelation to his soul. He stands at a crossroads of choice, as it were, of a path forward towards life and enlightenment, or backward towards confusion and darkness.

The Road Not Taken

By Robert Frost

Two roads diverged in a yellow wood,

And sorry I could not travel both

And be one traveler, long I stood

And looked down one as far as I could

To where it bent in the undergrowth;

Then took the other, as just as fair,

And having perhaps the better claim,

Because it was grassy and wanted wear;

Though as for that the passing there

Had worn them really about the same,

And both that morning equally lay

In leaves no step had trodden black.

Oh, I kept the first for another day!

Yet knowing how way leads on to way,

I doubted if I should ever come back.

I shall be telling this with a sigh

Somewhere ages and ages hence:

Two roads diverged in a wood, and I—

I took the one less traveled by,

And that has made all the difference.

It is a sacred and personal responsibility and choice for each person to choose the path to cultivate and honor the voice of truth to his soul, or to be led down the path of ignorance, confusion, deception, and falsehood.

In the final analysis, we are dependent upon the universal, omnipresent, varied and pervasive manifestations of God for truth. Our ability to find and discern truth will be dependent upon our willingness to hear and accept His manifestation of it.

> "My firm belief is that he reveals himself daily to every human being, but we shut our ears to the 'still small voice.' We shut our eyes to the pillar of fire in front of us... The divine music is incessantly going on within ourselves, but the loud senses drown the delicate music, which is unlike, and infinitely superior to, any we can perceive or hear with our senses."[38]   -- Gandhi

I have broken down reliable standards for truth as above in the interest of clarity and methodology. But this process becomes second nature to us more than we may realize. For example, in any argument that we are faced with, we naturally turn first to the known facts. Those known facts serve as the basis for rational discussion and argument. We interpret and organize those facts in reference to the basic principles that we are familiar with and ascribe to. Often, this is almost automatic to our consciousness. At this point, however, the difficulty often arises, and we can be left victims of our human limitations if we have not counseled the revelations of Deity. And so, confusion may persist on important controversies. If, at this point we are willing to look to divine revelation, clarity reasserts itself and knowledge can be affirmed from an unimpeachable source.

Simply yielding oneself with a deep, determined commitment to open his soul to the truth, to listen and follow the truth wherever it leads, will open and clarify the mind to discern truth in all of its radiant, sweet, and simple beauty. Like the bursting forth of the sun after the darkness and confusion of the storm, the light of truth brings freshness, peace, and illuminating comfort to a troubled soul.

Some persons choose not to accept facts, sound principles and values, or revelation from God: They are left without means to discover or determine truth. Then they are at the mercy of false standards, such as their passions, self-interest, and expediency, like a ship without a rudder in a troubled sea of confusion and doubt. As they turn to false standards of truth, inevitably the false standard fails, and ultimately, they are left in cynicism, darkness and despair, a slave to their own ignorance and pride.

6

False standards and impediments to discerning the truth

At any point in the search for truth, insidious pitfalls exist, so one must be vigilant to avoid deception by succumbing to false standards and real impediments to discerning truth.

Stereotypes commonly impose a false understanding of the truth. They offer a simplistic view of any particular person or idea, easy to accept, but wholly reprehensible as an opinion or belief based on prejudice and incomplete or inaccurate information.

Ideology can become an impediment to the truth when it mandates a commitment to a system of thought or philosophy that places loyalty to the entity at the expense of what is right, or what is true. We see this in the polarization of political parties in our day when loyalty to the party often supersedes what is best for the people. Then truth may be trampled in the interests of expediency.

Carried to the extreme, "Ideology...gives evildoing its long-sought justification and gives the evildoer the necessary steadfastness and determination... That was how the agents of the Inquisition fortified their wills: by invoking Christianity; the conquerors of foreign lands, by extolling the grandeur of their Motherland; the colonizers, by civilization; the Nazis, by race; and the Jacobins (early and late), by equality, brotherhood, and the happiness of future generations. Thanks to ideology, the twentieth century was fated to experience evildoing on a scale calculated in the millions."[39] --Solzhenitsyn

But we see this today as an ideology becomes dominant to the truth, and a substitute for individual inquiry and commitment to the truth. When one weds himself to an ideology, it's an easy way out from the work necessary to find and believe the truth.

Expediency--Sound principles trump expediency. In a tough spot, we are often tempted to turn to expediency at the expense of moral values and sound principles. "I abandoned free-market principles to save the free market," President George Bush famously stated during the financial market collapse of 2008, a clear abandonment of principle for expediency.

This easily morphs into "the end justifies the means", which may ultimately degenerate into catastrophic error and deception. The world's most horrific tragedies that have resulted in the murders of millions of people are the fruits of this pernicious doctrine, described by Jacob Bronowski, a contemporary scientist and author, as "... the belief that the end justifies the means... that push-button philosophy, that deliberate deafness to suffering, (that) has become the monster in the war machine. (This is)...the betrayal of the human spirit: the assertion of dogma that closes the mind, and turns a nation, a civilization, into a regiment of ghosts—obedient ghosts, or tortured ghosts."[40]

Opinion, or belief—Mere belief, or credibility, is not a reliable standard for truth. We often hear "I believe so-and-so..." in a controversy, based perhaps on the first blush exposure, or of what we want to believe, or what seems credible. We saw this recently in the US Senate hearings on the confirmation of a Supreme Court justice, when a character witness testified about the candidate's alleged sexual abuse. One of the senator's stated, "I believe you!" As if her belief established the witness's credibility. "...When proof is subordinated to mere belief, the standard for evidence is reduced to whatever bolsters the belief."[41] (--Jonah Goldberg) Belief can be bolstered by a multitude of (chosen) fanciful, fantastic, ephemeral and crazy ideas and imaginations.

"When politics becomes solely a matter of "I believe" versus "I believe," it descends into a raw contest for power. Historically, it's been fascists, not liberals, who tend to win such contests."[42] **--Bret Stephens**

"... statements on the controversy that begin, "I believe (so-and-so)" or "I believe (so-and-so)" — because they jibe with personal experience or align with a partisan motive — are empirically worthless and intellectually dishonest. I believe the defect could be corrected by saying, "I want to believe...."[43] -- Bret Stephens

Human reasoning—A man may imagine that his own, uninspired intellect alone is a reliable standard--what a stunning display of foolish arrogance![44] Human logic has historically and notoriously been subject to human fallibility. Unless tethered to reliable standards, human reasoning is fickle, capricious, and unreliable. (more in chapter 8, "Truth and Reason")

A portion of truth—So often we content ourselves with the portion of the truth that just fits our wants—only the part that makes us feel care-free and secure, and we settle for a few scraps at the grand feast, satiating our appetite with portions and remnants. We studiously avoid the whole meal, perhaps partaking of the most tasty delicacies, and that keeps us well-fed and comfortable, distracted and perhaps oblivious to the enjoyment of the complete feast of the knowledge of what is true. An example of this is the common assertion that one believes in an all-powerful force in the universe, without exploring the specifics of who/what that all-powerful force is. This tiny portion of the truth of the Deity enables one to acknowledge God, but not be held accountable to his commandments, and to avoid responsibility to live up to the grand destiny of the human race.

Counterfeit revelation--There are spiritual counterfeits to the revelations of God. One must be vigilant and very careful. Often, intense emotion is a handy vehicle for false revelation. One can be deceived by his own "want to believe" or "wishful thinking" if he does not carefully apply neutral and objective criteria to his belief. Even a focused mind may conjure up a false or desired "revelation." (See p 134 in chapter 16, "Strategies for Finding and Testing Truth for a personal example.) Usually, false revelation will appeal to carnal or selfish instincts, and will lead one away from his belief in God[45] and will be inconsistent with other revealed verities. We see this in occasional false leaders who claim special dispensation to release themselves from the standards of morality that everybody else is subject to.

In any specific situation, make sure that the standards of truth—facts, values and principles, established truth, the voice of conscience, and the revelations of God—all align and are consistent with each other. For example, a "revelation" that is contrary to core values, sound principles, or God's word to his prophets or in the scriptures, would be false. Likewise, a personal exemption from the standards that apply to everybody else would be suspect. A good example of this is the common mantra, "I have fallen in love with someone other than my spouse, with whom I have made sacred vows to be faithful." The value of loyalty to marriage covenants is inconsistent with the selfish desire for an illicit love affair. A "revelation" for an exemption from God-given moral standards applicable to everyone else is not consistent with truth. An "inspiration" that is at odds with known facts, values, and sound principles is not going to be consistent with truth.

False philosophies and religions have multiplied under the guise of truth. This has turned off many persons to the truthfulness and utility of religion, when it becomes patently obvious that superstition and dogma have intruded into the realm of reality and truth. Many religious sects possess elements of truth but are incomplete, lacking a "fullness of truth." Some have devolved and perverted the truth from an original, pure religion or creed. A religion and philosophy can be judged by not only the facts and principles upon which it is based, but also by its end-point: where does this philosophy lead? "By their fruits ye shall know them."[46]

True revealed religion is a divine message that transcends what one would call a "man-made" religious system. The revelation of the truthfulness of any specific religion is a personal imperative dependent only upon one's own enlightenment, and this cannot be imposed, forced or mandated by any other person or entity. (See chapter 12, "Truth and Religion.") It must be allowed, however, that the great religions of the world all contain elements of good (which speaks to a common origin). The decision of the truthfulness of any particular religion must remain an intimate, personal responsibility and decision, between the individual and God.

Another false philosophy is the so-called postmodern neomarxism (expounded brilliantly by Jordan Peterson[47]) which promotes relativism of all truth, equality of outcome, and interpretation of culture in terms of the oppressed and oppressors (power). Couched in the language of compassion and fairness, this philosophy breaks us down into interest groups pitted against one another and leads to intolerance, hatred, and violence. It has already resulted in the murders of millions of people in the twentieth century.

Pseudoscience is counterfeit science that starts with a false principle and then arranges or cherry-picks the facts to fit. It is a common source of falsity and deception, and is a great example of "motivated reasoning," which, rather than starting from a premise (hypothesis) and logically working one's way to a conclusion based on scientific observation, starts from a premise and a conclusion and then finds the reasons (facts) that connect the two. Often, the premise, or principle, is an idea that captivates the imagination and appeals to emotions and offers a simplistic explanation of a complex problem. The defect can be detected by application of sound principles backed up by evidence-based science (facts), with a rigorous adherence to the scientific method. (See chapter 16, "Truth and Science.") Again, the facts must align with sound principle for a reliable, truthful, conclusion. Although revelation is not a necessary ingredient of the scientific method, many great scientists have alluded to a spiritual enlightenment at times that have led them to the discovery of important scientific principles.

Doubt. Do not doubt the revelation of God to your soul.[48] After you have carefully purified your intent, distinguished your bias and emotion from your authentic inner voice, and banished false standards for belief, you will have confidence to look forward and upward with faith, not backward in doubt.

The search for truth will be aided by a diligent, careful, and sincere application of reliable standards and a rejection of false standards. This process may engender anxiety, become strenuous, and even fearful. It will be a gauntlet of searching, self-discovery, repentance, sacrifice, and recalibration. Honest introspection may lead to a painful, yet valuable, and liberating, discovery, as one lets go of the false, and embraces the true.

See Chapter 17, "Strategies for Finding and Testing Truth" for specific suggestions.

Oh Say, What Is Truth?

By John Jaques

Oh Say, what is truth? 'Tis the fairest gem

That the riches of worlds can produce,

And priceless the value of truth will be when

The proud monarch's costliest diadem

Is counted but dross and refuse.

Yes, say, what is truth? 'Tis the brightest prize

To which mortals or Gods can aspire;

Go search in the depths where it glittering lies

Or ascend in pursuit to the loftiest skies.

'Tis an aim for the noblest desire.

The scepter may fall from the despot's grasp

When with winds of stern justice he copes,

But the pillar of truth will endure to the last,

And its firm-rooted bulwarks outstand the rude blast,

And the wreck of the fell tyrant's hopes.

Then say, what is truth: 'Tis the last and the first,

For the limits of time it steps o'er.

Though the heavens depart and the earth's fountains burst,

Truth, the sum of existence, will weather the worst,

Eternal, unchanged, evermore.[49]

My Discovery of Truth

My own experience

My discovery of truth began in childhood years, grew with fits and starts into adolescence, gained momentum with confirmation in young manhood, extended through the early years of marriage and rearing a family, was severely tested with adversity in mid-life, and has crystallized in mature years. It was a process that began as small moments of learning at my mother's knee, obedience as a child to my parents, and then perceptibly gained ground with life experiences, setbacks, mistakes, experimentation, repenting, recalibration, testing, and finally, fulfillment in maturity as a miracle of understanding and confidence. Step-by-step, line-upon-line. precept-upon-precept.

As a child, I was reared in a devoutly religious home and taught the values and principles of the Christian religion. I accepted these values and principles as a child and young man with an inherent and natural desire to do what is right. It was a great blessing to have goodly parents who taught me the importance of honesty, belief in God, and in always doing what is right. So, these things came naturally to me. But that is different from a personal knowledge. As a teenager I felt compelled to know the truth of these things for myself. I had already experienced the value of honesty and clean living, but as far as the existence of God and the truth of the Christian religion, I wanted to know it for myself, independently of the traditions of my family and the Church I grew up in.

I thus embarked on a course of study of religions and related scriptures and teachings. I found truth and goodness in all of the religions I studied, but particularly it was easy for me to see the truth of my own religion. I must confess that the truth of these things seemed obvious and easy to my intellect. It all made sense to me. But that is different from a spiritual knowledge of the truth of all of that. I realized that I needed more than the traditions of my fathers and the teachings of my youth. I had been taught to pray and ask God about the truth of such things, so I, believing in God, decided that I must have a personal knowledge. I thence found a private time and place to ask God if the things I had been taught were true.

I still remember the time and setting of that event: a beautiful Spring morning in the mountains of Idaho, where I was working for the US Forest Service spraying trees for a bug infestation. I walked up the hill behind our camp in the pine forest, knelt, and asked God if what I had been taught was true. As I prayed, I heard no voice, but a powerful, sweet, enlightenment enveloped me that confirmed that what I had been taught was indeed true. I cannot explain this experience in terms of my physical senses, but an inner peace and confidence replaced doubt. This experience I remember as brightly and clearly now as the day it happened many years ago. I look back and see this experience as the principle basis of my belief in what is true. It confirmed to me that revelation is indeed real and can be relied upon. While I certainly did not know the truth of all things, I knew the truth of this thing, and it gave me confidence to move forward with faith and patience in living the Christian life. From the knowledge of this one truth, I could thence conclude the truth of a cascade of related things. I knew that God was real, and that He would answer my prayers. I felt His Spirit and influence in a subtle but powerful way that changed my heart—I could never deny the reality of that moment.

This experience became the model for me in searching for truth: careful investigation and study of facts, identifying basic values and principles, and seeking my own revelation for what is true. The spiritual experience was one of enlightenment and surety, a still, small voice within that has never since failed.

8

Truth and Reason

"But to be learned is good if they hearken unto the counsels of God."

-- Book of Mormon, 2 Nephi 9:29

"Arguments, like men, are often pretenders."

--Plato

God has given man a mind, and He expects men to use their mind and rational powers of reasoning to the fullest. As sincere seekers for truth counsel together, explore diverse opinions and experiences, consider opposing arguments, and open their minds and hearts to truth, much insight, wisdom, and truth abound50. Indeed, for sincere seekers of truth who look to God, He enlightens their minds and expands their intellect to the discovery and understanding of truth in a magnificent revelatory panorama of distinctive and universal truth. Thus, human reasoning should be a spiritual, as well as purely a physical, process. It is only when the arrogance of human reasoning takes honor unto itself alone, abandoning the wisdom and revelations of God, whatever form they may take, that the human intellect becomes arid and fruitless. Conversely, when the revelations of God are deformed, perverted into dogmatic assertions that make no sense, sullied with the philosophies and prevarications of men, they darken and stultify the intellect and enlightenment of the soul.

Scholars and intellectual seekers have sought truth through the ages. The great thinkers have attempted to solve the problems of human existence through exhaustive study and human reasoning. This has resulted in a multitude of philosophies and systems of thought. But, despite prodigious and comprehensive efforts to formulate a universal philosophy their efforts have ended as a shadow--futile and fruitless in the grand search for the fullness of truth, works that torture language and thought in a complex morass of bewilderment, perplexity, and confusion. Such are the works of the uninspired human mind.

Hugh Nibley, professor of ancient history at Brigham Young University, an acclaimed professor of ancient history, said it this way:

> "In the realm of the mind, in letters, the arts, and in most of the sciences, it was the ancient Greeks, most educated people will concede, who walked off with nearly all the first prizes. It is hard to say anything on any but the most specialized and technical of matters that some Greek many centuries ago did not say better. If any people ever knew and lived life well and fully, it was the chosen spirits among the Greeks. They explored every avenue of human experience; they inquired into every possibility of broadening and improving the mind; they sought the truth as persistently and as honestly as men can ever be expected to seek; and, sounding the depths and skirting the outmost bounds of man's wisdom, came to the unanimous conclusion that the wisdom of man is as nothing." [51]

The futility of discovering truth by reason alone is aptly manifested by the efforts of the Christian apologists to clear up doctrinal controversies in the early Christian Church after the death of the Apostles, when the era of revelation had ended in the Church. While the Apostles lived, they enjoyed not only their own personal relationship with Jesus Christ but were promised and were given the Gift of the Holy Ghost, which revelation was an active and ongoing process in managing the affairs of the Church after his death. After the Apostles died, the Church no longer had access to this revelation, and was left to the reasoning and opinions of uninspired men. It is clear from the writings of the early Church fathers that they realized this, and sorely lamented the loss. Clement of Alexandria, a Christian convert, writes in his Clementine Recognitions, "Wishing to learn something, I frequented the schools of the philosophers, where, however, I heard nothing but dogmatic assertions and equally dogmatic refutations endlessly put forth—formal disputations, artfully constructed syllogisms, and subtle conclusions... Neither side ever brought forth proof that really convinced me inside, because the statements and definitions of things passes as true or false not from the actual nature of things or the real truth, but always according to the skill and cleverness of the people putting them forth." (In Clement's)..."first gospel conversation with Peter, Peter compares the world in which we live to a great house filled with dense smoke—blinding smoke produced by human unbelief, malice, ambition, greed, etc. Because of this smoke, the people who live in the house can see nothing clearly, but we must imagine them groping about with weak and running eyes, coughing and scolding, bumping into each other, tripping over furniture, trying to make out a bit of reality here and there—a corner, a step, a wall—and then trying to fit their desperate and faulty data together to make some kind of sense".... "Justin... saw clearly that only by revelation from outside could man be freed from his fearful confinement within the narrow cell of his own limited experience... Origen compares the human intellect at its brilliant best with a tiny little candle, a feeble spark that can hardly light a foot of the way ahead. And Tertullian likens the philosophers to men stumbling and groping about in the dark. Once in a while, he says, they do 'stumble on the truth by a happy accident...'"[52]

Perhaps the greatest of all the Christian intellectuals, St. Augustine, is credited with establishing the Christian Church on a solid foundation of rational thought. His is an example of substituting human thought and intellect for revelation. The revelatory traditions of the pristine Church had been lost, and he tackled the impossible job of harmonizing the spiritual doctrines of Christ with the wisdom of men. He never solved the thorny doctrinal questions facing the Church, such as the true nature of the Godhead, the function of the Holy Ghost, and the doctrine of repentance and forgiveness of sins.[53] Another influential thinker of the early Christian church was Origen, who is credited by creating the doctrinal theology of the Church. However, on these first principles of the gospel such as the Spirit of God, the Holy Ghost, resurrected bodies, he is unable to find any definitive answer. "On all these points and many more, Origen, the foremost doctrinal authority in the church, has no certitude and claims no authority—and this on themes which lie according to his own assertion at the very heart of doctrine, the first principles of the gospel... There never was, indeed, it is hard to imagine how there could be, a more zealous, devout, single-minded student than Origen, nicknamed Adamantinos, 'the unshakable.' Born and reared in a school, he was convinced that all knowledge of the gospel could be acquired by study alone and only ended up proving to the world that where there is no revelation there is no certitude."[54]

> "It has been increasingly recognized in recent years that the ritual and liturgy of the Church was actually a substitute for the lost charismatic gifts; the mass thus presents the ultimate paradox, a controlled miracle, in which the priest does everything but actually does nothing."[55]

Even the Father of Philosophy, Plato, acknowledged the futility of intellect without revelation: "... we must declare that this Cosmos has verily come into existence as a Living Creature endowed with soul and reason owing to the providence of God."[56] And, "Concerning the soul, then what part of it is mortal, what part immortal, and where and with what companions and for what reasons these have been housed apart, only if God concurred could we dare to affirm that our account is true."[57]

And yet, wise and humble thinkers have always found elements of truth as they humbly looked beyond their own intellect and consulted the works and laws of God. Indeed, the cultural, scientific, and political traditions of Western culture that contributed to our present freedom and prosperity are built on the spiritual, intellectual and academic foundations these giants of human thought have bequeathed to humanity. When their thinking was in line with and consistent with God's law, they were able to elucidate profound wisdom and truth.

> "Men of an extraordinary success, in their honest moments, have always sung 'Not unto us, not unto us.' According to the faith of their times they have built altars to Fortune, or to Destiny, or to St. Julian. Their success lay in their parallelism to the course of thought, which found in them an unobstructed

channel; and the wonders of which they were the visible conductors seemed to the eye their deed.... That which externally seemed will and immovableness was willingness and self-annihilation."[58] -- Ralph Waldo Emerson, "Spiritual Laws"

A great example of this is the establishment of the principles of government and liberty by the founders of our Nation. Probably never before had such a unique group of individuals of experience, character, and intellect been gathered together for the great task that lay before them. The founders of our nation relied heavily on human reasoning, as well as on divine help in formulating the documents of Liberty and Freedom and our Constitution. At the Constitutional Convention of 1787, at a moment of difficulty and impasse, the venerable Benjamin Franklin arose and addressed himself to Washington in the chair, "The small progress we have made after four or five weeks close attendance and continual reasonings with each other—our different sentiments on almost every question ... producing almost as many noes as ayes, is methinks a melancholy proof of the imperfection of the human understanding. We indeed seem to feel our own want of political wisdom, since we have been running about in search of it. We have gone back to ancient history for models of government, and examined the different forms of those republics which, having been formed with the seeds of their own dissolution, now no longer exist... In this situation of this assembly, groping as it were in the dark to find political truth, and scarce able to distinguish it when presented to us, how has it happened, Sir, that we have not hitherto once thought of humbly applying to the Father of lights to illuminate our understandings?" He reminded the Convention how at the beginning of the war with England, the Continental Congress had had prayers for divine protection—and in this very room. "Our prayers, Sir, were heard, and they were graciously answered. All of us who were engaged in the struggle must have observed frequent instances of a Superintending providence in our favor. To that kind providence we owe this happy opportunity of consulting in peace on the means of establishing our future national felicity. And have we now forgotten that powerful friend?... I have lived, Sir, a long time and the longer I live, the more convincing proofs I see of this truth—that God governs in the affairs of men. And if a sparrow cannot fall to the ground without his notice, is it probable that an empire can rise without his aid? ... I therefore beg leave to move—that henceforth prayers imploring the assistance of Heaven, and its blessings on our deliberations, be held in this Assembly every morning before we proceed to business."[59]

These men were practiced and educated in the great intellectual and philosophical traditions of Western culture. They relied on a tradition embodied in the philosophy of John Locke, "Natural Law." By consulting the laws of Nature and the laws of God, and weaving them inextricably together, they discovered that Natural Law is really an extension of God's law, so that, although specific revelation to particular circumstances is not always essential to reasoning, when human reasoning follows Natural Law, it is fully consistent with God's Law. Alexander Hamilton said that Natural Law, that part of the law of God that reason can allow us to understand through rational faculties He gave us, is higher than human law.[60]   Indeed, the Spirit of God speaks to humans through enlightenment of their minds, so that human reasoning when consistent with God's Law is really just another form of revelation.

Yes, reason is essential. But when human reasoning abandons the counsels of God, humans are left to their own short-sightedness and intellectual weakness and are at the mercy of the futility of their own myopic view and opinion.

"There is something infinitely higher than intellect that rules us, as even the skeptics. Their skepticism and philosophy do not help them in the critical period of their lives. They need something better, something outside them. And so, if someone puts a conundrum before me, I say to him, "You are not going to know the meaning of God or prayer unless you reduce yourself to a cipher. You must be humble enough to see that in spite of your greatness and gigantic intellect you are but a speck in the universe. A merely intellectual conception of things of life is not enough. It is the spiritual conception which eludes the intellect, and which alone can give one satisfaction...

"Intellect takes along, in the battle of life, to a certain extent, but at the crucial moment fails us. Faith transcends reason. It is when the horizon is the darkest and our human reason is beaten down to the ground, that faith shines the brightest and comes to our rescue. It is such faith that our youth requires and this comes when one has shed all pride of intellect and surrendered oneself entirely to his will."[61]—Gandhi

Thus, we see that inspired human reasoning is an essential process in discovering truth.   The pitfall of worshipping one's own intellect, however, by substituting uninspired reason for revelation, leads to catastrophic error and confusion. We must remember that the human mind is ultimately dependent on revelation for enlightenment and for the crucial spiritual knowledge of human existence and destiny. "Using our mind without our heart will not bring spiritual answers."[62] The scripture aptly concludes, "O the vainness, and the frailties, and the foolishness of men! When they are learned they think they are wise, and they hearken not unto the counsel of God, for they set it aside, supposing they know of themselves, wherefore, their wisdom is foolishness and it profiteth them not. And they shall perish. But to be learned is good if they hearken unto the counsels of God."[63]

The Death of Reason

The age-old experiments of human intellect and reasoning failed to provide the existential answers to human life and meaning. Scholar after scholar, philosopher after philosopher, each providing perhaps part of the answer, failed in formulating a comprehensive philosophy of truth. Much has been said of the Enlightenment, which enshrined the western tradition of rational thinking and analysis. Without discounting the prodigious accomplishments of rational thinking in the domains of science and technology, let it be admitted that philosophy, in answering the moral and spiritual questions of man, his origin and destiny, has been an utter failure.

And so we have come full circle from the ancient Greeks, who concluded millennia ago, that, according to Pyrrho of Elis, "Neither the senses nor reason can give us sure knowledge: the senses distort the object in perceiving it, and reason is merely the sophist servant of desire. Every syllogism begs the question, for its major premise assumes its conclusion. 'Every reason has a corresponding reason opposed to it'..."[64] The acclaimed historian, Will Durant, concluded that "The age of the great systems gave way to doubt in the ability of reason either to understand the world or to control the impulses of men into order and civilization... Philosophy... gave up the pursuit of truth and the quest of happiness..."[65]

So, our generation is still trying to formulate intellectual philosophies that work, and in their compulsion to find a new way that does work, is jettisoning reason:

> "Unfortunately, reason is no longer in vogue... Subjectivity rules the day... Reason, in fact, is insulting. Reason suggests that one person can know better than another, that one person's perspective can be more correct than someone else's. Reason is intolerant. Reason demands standards. Better to destroy reason than to abide by its dictates.
>
> "... The death of reason could have been predicted once reason alone failed to provide us with meaning." [66] --Ben Shapiro

To replace the futile philosophies of reason, our own generation is exploring a new way of thinking, one based not on reason, but on primitive and tribal values of self-protection and self-interest alone, with power as the principal arbiter. This narcissistic philosophy claims that each person has his own interest, his own truth, and deserves credence for his actions/self-fulfillment just because it is his own way, or his own "truth". (There is a difference between accepting with respect how people are and giving credence to their views.) In conjunction with the leftist postmodern neomarxist philosophy that promotes equality at the expense of liberty, power instead ethics, we see on display the increasing intolerance of alternate viewpoints that renders rational discussion impossible. This, then, frequently fosters violence in an effort to shut down free (opposing) speech (the Antifa movement). This could have been predicted, however, because the new philosophy is just a variation of the totalitarian Marxist and fascist philosophies of the twentieth century. There is no tolerance for opposing viewpoints, because "I" have the power to decide that "I am right, and you are wrong. This is my truth!" No place for established values and sound principles here. This is the dangerous new (old) philosophy of our day that threatens the very foundations of liberty and the Judeo-Christian ethics of our culture.

This new philosophy is insidious and destructive. It sees the values and principles built upon millennia of human experience and the revelations of God as merely tools of an elite minority to enshrine their power at the expense of the many. Granted, the failure of reason to provide the real answers, and the failure of corrupted institutions lends credence to the disillusionment of the cynical and disenchanted. But, in counterbalance to that, the triumph of virtue and liberty in the world today (the rapid development of free societies and governments in the 19th and 20th centuries, and the spread of democracy) reflects fundamental progress and truth. The solution then is not to tear down the system and return us to the dark ages, but to reform and build on correct values and principles, with revelation as a guide.

This destructive thinking is why we can't reason with each other anymore. This is why rational discussion is no longer possible. This is why we seem hopelessly polarized.

This is what happens when reason is uncoupled from revelation. We are left at the mercy of our passions and animal instincts of self-preservation, false and corrupted ideologies, and we dive to the degenerate, tribal, power-centered, chaotic state of mankind. This has happened before.

This modernized version of an ancient, debunked and discredited, and, yes, fatal, philosophy, must be seen for what it is. It must be fought and defeated if our civilization is to survive.

9

A Season of Adversity and Testing

A personal journey

I learned the futility of my own reasoning when mid-life crisis hit me like a Mac truck. I had a wonderful family with seven beautiful children, a thriving medical career, and community respect, in short, a life without vice. I became overconfident with all this success, in retrospect, and ventured to experiment a little too close to the edge of the cliff of acceptable behavior. I started to cultivate thoughts that would be unworthy of a faithful husband, father, and churchgoer. I thought I could handle this myself, but it set me up for the inevitable fall when confronted with explicit temptation, and I fell head-long into the vice of adultery. I knew it was wrong, but I consoled myself with, "it won't last long," and "I can extricate myself after just a few dalliances." I soon rationalized myself into "I don't love my wife anymore," and "I have a right to be happy" with relationships outside of my marriage vows. This led to separation and eventual divorce. Then, I thought, I would be free to live the life that I expected would be fulfilling and happy. But it just didn't stop there. I fell into a true downward spiral into actions of decadent immorality. Far from finding fulfillment and happiness, I could not rid myself from the unrelenting and enveloping sense of guilt and emptiness, although I had another fine relationship that seemed to be working. I rationalized that with time, I could find peace. But, rather, contentment and peace were ever more elusive. I would delve into physical pleasures only to feel, after a weekend of fun, remorse and a penetrating sense of wanting to be extricated. In the meantime, I had ended my marriage, lost the trust and confidence of my children, and lost my membership in my church. These I thought would be worth the gain of a relationship that I had always wanted and craved. But there was no happiness, only temporary pleasure, followed by an inevitable let-down. I had lost my honor.

In the midst of this unhappiness that was overtaking me, one night as I was going to bed I felt the urge to kneel in prayer to my Heavenly Father, and I felt and expressed the desire of my heart to tell Him that, "I want to be a good man!" Immediately, I could feel Him say to me, in my mind's eye, "Tom, you are a good man!" This was clear and undeniable. It spoke to my inner self with a power that I have never forgotten. I knew from that moment that God knew me and loved me, and that I was good inside. He had not condemned me. I powerfully felt the love of God. But I also perceived that I must end my life of wrongful actions and make things right with my family and with my church with full accountability. I was constrained to be honest with myself and face the reality of my betrayal of my own conscience and knowledge of what is right and what is wrong. This was a painful realization.

But my lifestyle had a grip on me that was not easy to break. I kept going back, ever with a resolve to not participate in immoral behavior, but always falling right back in, with a promise that next time, "we could just be friends." This never worked.

I remember flying back from one of these weekends (I had to return for work), when a sudden, distinct enlightenment and understanding descended upon me: "This relationship you have is something, but it is not love—and it will bring you no happiness." I then knew that I had to end the illicit relationship. I sought help from my Bishop and returned to daily prayer and church attendance. But I was still weak, relying on my own strength to figure it all out and overcome the weaknesses of the flesh that I was subject to. I could not seem to find the strength to completely end the relationship. I felt obligated by friendship, even though I now see that it was not real friendship, but lust and selfishness. This illicit relationship had such a hold on me that it took me fully two years to completely extricate myself from it. I learned that I had no power of myself when exposed to the wrong environment.

During these months, I struggled with the concepts of truth, the moral standard, and how to find power to overcome my addiction (for this had all the landmarks of an addiction). Who can set the moral standard? Who can decisively state what is right and what is wrong? Why can't I find the power within to overcome my weakness? I went back to the teachings of my parents when I was a child, and the doctrine of Jesus Christ and his Atonement. I realized that I knew these things but had not fully internalized them and practiced them. I had left out some key elements in my understanding and actions. In this turmoil of mind, I finally concluded that I would simply accept the Prophet's declaration as the word of God that my actions were wrong. This was a key decision, for it opened to me the next resolution, that I could practice obedience to the commandments of God, and simply give up my wrong acts. In doing this, I had to give up some of my most cherished beliefs, my most wanted actions, and look higher for the wisdom and power to change. I realized that I didn't have the power to change my bad desires, but that I could give up the bad actions, and then pray that God would change my heart. I then began to pray to God for strength to stay on this path of repentance.

This worked! It's the only thing that ever did work for me in this respect! It not only worked, but I experienced a spiritual conversion and witness that it was true.

I embarked on the journey and finally gained the power to completely forsake the illicit relationship and my unworthy and bad actions. This opened the door for reconciliation to my wife, and restoration of the trust and confidence of my children. This required full honesty, accountability, and a willingness on my part to give up my vices in the interest of what is right. We have since been remarried, reconciled with my children, and restored to full fellowship in my church. And life is wonderful again. I have my honor back!

I am so grateful for the forgiveness of my family, for their patience and long-suffering, as well of that of my Heavenly Father, and for the redeeming power of the Atonement of Jesus Christ which delivered me from the abyss of sin and saved me.

It is from this experience that I have worked out the elements of this book—how to seek, discover, and embrace the truth. I learned that I had the power to give up my wrongful thoughts and actions through simple obedience to the commandments of God. I learned to distinguish my natural inclinations and bias from the still, small voice of revelation from God to me in a most personal way. When no other man could answer and help the predicament I was in, I heard the voice of God to my heart, and learned the wisdom that no man could tell me. I learned to hear and trust that voice, and it has brought peace, comfort, and the indescribable joy of achieving self-mastery. Indeed, the truth has made me free.

This experience led directly to the insights, understanding, and my ability to write the next chapter, "Truth and Personal Behavior." The comprehension of these important concepts may seem intellectually obvious to some, but for me, it came from my own raw, agonizing, painful, yet liberating, experience.

10

Truth and Personal Behavior

"let it begin with me"

"Character is the habit of action
from the permanent vision of truth.
It carries a superiority to all the accidents of life."[67]
-- Ralph Waldo Emerson

It was a bright November Fall morning and the sun was just rising over the horizon, casting shadows from the East in the glory of a beautiful and fresh new day. I was driving my Ford pickup homeward after a night working in the Emergency Room. Election day had just occurred, and my thoughts were a thicket of wonder and confusion at the outcome. "How was it possible that a majority of the country had voted for the candidate that I viewed as the wrong one?" "How was it possible that some of my wonderful, good friends saw the election issues completely different than I?" I had studied carefully the issues of the election and felt confident that I had made a good voting choice. How could it be that so many of the individuals in our country saw it differently?

As the beauty and stillness of the cool and clear autumn morning settled around me, a sudden, external enlightenment enveloped me, and I could see and comprehend a crucial truth: *"If a man is not honest about the most personal and intimate aspects of his own life, he is vulnerable to deception."* At this moment, I learned this truth from the inside out, an epiphany of insight that explains so much of why we are not unified as a people. This was not a judgment of other people and their motives, for I am not a judge of others, but it illuminated to me the vital importance of being honest with myself in an ongoing process of self-examination.

One must have pure motives and real intent to consistently discern truth. It has been my experience that one's ability to discern, understand, believe in, and embrace the truth is largely based upon his choice to accept and obey the truth about his own life, even in the little details, those which may seem insignificant, but which over time form a pattern of character. Will he be honest with himself?

If a man is not honest about the most personal and intimate aspects of his own life, he is vulnerable to deception. His motives will not be pure until he has given up conflicted interests, desires and dishonorable actions in the search for truth. For, until he does, he will be justifying or defending his own wrong behavior, instead of dispassionately seeking the truth. Neither will he be confident of his perception of truth until he has aligned his personal behavior with virtue and uprightness. As Emerson so eloquently stated,

> "When we break the laws, we lose our hold on the central reality...
>
> "In this kingdom of illusions we grope eagerly for stays and foundations. There is none but a strict and faithful dealing at home, and a severe barring out of all duplicity or illusion there. Whatever games are played with us, we must play no games with ourselves, but deal in our privacy with the last honesty and truth. I look upon the simple and childish virtues of veracity and honesty as the root of all that is sublime in character. Speak as you think, be what you are, pay your debts of all kinds. I prefer to be owned as sound and solvent, and my word as good as my bond, and to be what cannot be skipped, or dissipated, or undermined, to all the éclat of the universe. This reality is the foundation of friendship, religion, poetry, and art..."[68]

This is why the pursuit of truth leads to God. Gandhi, that prophet for his time stated, "Truth and righteousness must forever remain the law in God's world... Character is based on virtuous action, and virtuous action is grounded on truth. Truth, then, is the source and foundation of all things that are good and great.[69]

The virtue, or righteousness, that is essential to our enlightenment of truth, springs from our willingness to be obedient to the laws of the universe, or to the laws of God. This is an act of self-surrender, of sacrifice, of complete honesty and commitment to the truth. It prepares our hearts for a great outpouring of illumination and power.

> "...there is one right act—that of self-surrender—which cannot be willed to the height by fallen creatures unless it is unpleasant. And ...this one right act includes all other righteousness, and the supreme cancelling of Adam's fall, the movement 'full speed astern' by which we retrace our long journey from Paradise, the untying of the old, hard knot, must be when the creature, with no desire to aid it, stripped naked to the bare willing of obedience, embraces what is contrary to its nature, and does that for which only one motive is possible. Such an act may be described as a 'test' of the creature's return to God: hence our fathers said that troubles were 'sent to try us'".[70] -- C.S. Lewis

When we break away from God and the moral law, we break away from real life, and lose the power to discern reality. As we cut ourselves loose from moral restraint and suffer our prejudices, vices and passions to control our behavior, we enslave ourselves in mists of illusion and darkness, and lose the power to spiritually discern truth.

This does not mean that we have to be perfect to find truth. But it does mean that we must be on the path of repentance and righteousness in an ongoing process of self-examination, exerting our best efforts on our daily journey towards virtue.

Relationships

Nowhere is this truer than in our dealings with each other. The same challenge to see things as they really are is so crucial to our relationships with our loved ones, spouses, friends, and even our enemies. This is the great challenge of life: to see what really is, to see the truth of what is, in every circumstance, and with every person. In this respect, our families are great repositories of truth. As James Q. Wilson wrote: "We learn to cope with the people of this world because we learn to cope with the members of our family. Those who flee the family flee the world; bereft of the (family's) affection, tutelage, and challenges, they are unprepared for the (world's) tests, judgments, and demands."71 As we learn and apply the principles of kindness, patience, and forgiveness, we become freed of our hurts, offenses, and pride. As we give up our preconceived and stereotypical notions, fears, and hasty judgments, we will be able to see persons as they really are and treat them with love and respect. These truths free us from misunderstanding and contention. This is one of the greatest victories of truth.

My search for truth has been an essentially religious experience (for the essence of truth is divine), in combination with life experience, careful observation and study. I have learned that to know truth I have to be living compatible with the laws of the universe.

11

Nature and Truth

Symbols of truth

...so shalt thou see and hear

The lovely shapes and sounds intelligible

Of that eternal language, which thy God

Utters, who from eternity doth teach

Himself in all, and all things in himself.

Great universal Teacher![72]

--Samuel Taylor Coleridge, "Frost at Midnight"

Nature is the Great Teacher.

Nature is a powerful force for teaching us of the laws of the universe. Here we see in full and awesome display the essence of the laws of cause and effect, the discipline of obedience, and the magnificence and glory of truth.

Look around you. Absorb the essence of Nature's message to you. As you train your eyes to see, and your ears to hear, you will find your spirit inspired, intellect expanded, your thought clarified, and your understanding of truth magnified. Nature is the perfect setting for the distillation of truth to the human soul.

What is it about Nature that leaves us with a sense of the sublime, of the beautiful, of the powerful, that seems to transcend our daily existence? We are led to the mountain peaks and canyons, the hills and woods and trees, spring pastures with carpets of wildflowers, a mighty river flowing to the sea; the sea with teaming, colorful, endless variety of exquisite life, a tropical rainforest studded with brilliant and varied birds, butterflies and flowers. We find Nature in our backyard in the shade of the oak tree on a hot summer's afternoon. We find her in a moist summer's evening as the fireflies rise in an evanescent spectacle of a multitude of glowing fairy lights. We find her in the clear, night sky, amid stars innumerable as the sands of the sea, all cast as stunning, natural loveliness that powerfully impresses our souls with the melody of indescribable beauty and universal life.

The variety of the forms of nature is inexhaustible. Each form is exquisite and unique. Yet, each carries a suggestion of kinship to the rest. Basic elements and consistent patterns suggest a common origin. All of the forms of nature exhibit purposefulness. As we examine closely, we find the relatedness and fragile interdependency of the natural world. Even in the violence and death of the terrestrial world, we find beauty and completeness in the never-ending cycle of Life that emerges from moldering mortality and that makes all wrongs right.

We are incapable of full appreciation, full completeness with Nature. We cannot quite take it all in. We want more—but the more we find, the more there is. Surely, we feel that we are "strangers and foreigners" in this world. And yet, amidst the sublime beauty and power of nature, we are constrained to acknowledge that our own experience suggests to our hearts and holds the promise of Life in greater majesty, beauty, and power than we have ever dreamt. It points us forward and upward: "Eye hath not seen, nor heard, nor hath it entered into the heart of man..."[73] The images of Nature are symbolic of that promise.

Byrd in Antarctica

In the winter of 1934, Admiral Richard E. Byrd set out on an adventure to set up a weather station deep in Antarctica, where he spent the dark Antarctic winter alone.

"... Freed from materialistic distractions, my senses sharpened in new directions, and the random or commonplace affairs of the sky and the earth and the spirit, which ordinarily I would have ignored if I had noticed them at all, became exciting and portentous...

"I am finding that life here has become largely a life of the mind. Unhurried reflection is a sort of companion. Yes, solitude is greater than I anticipated. My sense of values is changing, and many things which before were in solution in my mind now seem to be crystallizing. I am better able to tell what in the world is wheat for me and what is chaff. In fact, my definition of success itself is changing. Just lately my views about man and his place in the cosmic scheme have begun to run something like this: If I had never seen a watch and should see one for the first time, I should be sure its hands were moving according to some plan and not at random. Nor does it seem any more reasonable for me to conceive that the precision and order of the universe is the product of blind chance. This whole concept is summed up on the word harmony. For those who seek it, there is inexhaustible evidence of an all-pervading intelligence.

"The human race, my intuition tells me, is not outside the cosmic process and is not an accident. It is as much a part of the universe as the trees, the mountains, the aurora, and the stars. My reason approves this; and the findings of science, as I see them, point in the same direction...

"Therefore, it seems to me that convictions of right and wrong, being, as they are, products of the consciousness, must also be formed in accordance with these laws. I believe further that the age-tested convictions of right and wrong... are as much a manifestation of cosmic law and intelligence as are all other phenomena..."[74]

This is a great example of how Nature can teach us fundamental verities about ourselves, our place in the universe, and our duty as human beings in a sublime setting of peace and harmony.

"The peace I describe is not passive. It must be won. Real peace comes from struggle that involves such things as effort, discipline, enthusiasm. This is also the way to strength...

"When a man achieves a fair measure of harmony within himself and his family circle, he achieves peace; and a nation made up of such individuals and groups is a happy nation. As the harmony of a star in its course is expressed by rhythm and grace, so the harmony of a man's life-course is expressed by happiness; this, I believe, is the prime desire of mankind."[75]

While suffering the effects of chronic carbon monoxide poisoning, he became very ill:

"...Great waves of fear, a fear I had never known before swept through me and settled deep within. But it wasn't the fear of suffering or even of death itself. It was a terrible anxiety over the consequences to those at home if I failed to return... During those hours of bitterness, I saw my whole life pass in review. I realized how wrong my sense of values had been and how I had failed to see that the simple, homely unpretentious things of life are the most important.

"At the end only two things really matter to a man, regardless of who he is; and they are the affection and understanding of his family. Anything and everything else he creates are insubstantial; they are ships given over to the mercy of the winds and tides of prejudice. But the family is an everlasting anchorage, a quiet harbor where a man's ships can be left to swing to the moorings of pride and loyalty."[76]

This man was taught as he purified and focused his mind in the silence and grandeur of Nature. This hearkens back to my own love of Nature and the realization that my family relationships were of inestimable value when I had betrayed them and was at risk at losing them forever. (See Chapter 8, "A Season of Adversity and Testing").

Nature teaches us that there is a Creator, a God, for all things in Nature testify of Him.   I have had the same experience as Abraham Lincoln when I have beheld the wonders of Nature.

> "I never behold them (the heavens filled with stars) that I do not feel I am
> looking into the face of God. I can see how it might be possible for a man to look
> down upon the earth and be an atheist, but I cannot conceive how he could look
> up into the heavens and say there is no God".

Symbols of truth

These manifestations of Nature expressed as beautiful and sublime images, sensations, stirring and inspiring thoughts and feelings, can be integrated into our very being as we recognize them as *symbols* of truth, of the reality of universal and eternal life, of infinite goodness and love.

This beautiful poem by my friend David Gatten is a perfect example of how the images of Nature are symbolic of eternal realities:

On these days,

when the clouds so clearly bear

likeness to the battlements of heaven,

one could scarcely feign

surprise

were they to part

and the very sky behind them

was replaced

with the great gates themselves.[77]

This beauty of Nature holds a semblance to a higher and more pure and holy reality. Plato recognized this in this beautiful rendition from "The Symposium:"

"This, my dear Socrates, ... is that life above all others which man should live, in the contemplation of beauty absolute; a beauty which if you once beheld, you would see not to be after the measure of gold, and garments, ... if man had eyes to see the true beauty--the divine beauty, I mean, pure and clear and unalloyed, not clogged with the portions of mortality and all the colors and vanities of human life--thither looking, and holding converse with the true beauty simple and divine? Remember how in that communion only, beholding beauty with the eye of the mind, he will be enabled to bring forth, not images of beauty, but realities (for he has hold not of an image but of a reality), and bringing forth and nourishing true virtue to become the friend of God and be immortal, if mortal man may...

"... the true order of going... is to begin from the beauties of earth and mount upwards for the sake of that other beauty, using these as steps only, and from one going on to two, and from two to all fair forms, and from fair forms to fair practices, and from fair practices to fair notions, until from fair notions he arrives at the notion of absolute beauty, and at last knows what the essence of beauty is."[78]

Emerson described this beauty of Nature as a symbol and a pathway to virtue.

"The ancient Greeks called the world beauty... The presence of a higher, namely, of the spiritual element is essential to its perfection. The high and divine beauty which can be loved without effeminacy, is that which can be found in combination with the human will & never separate. Beauty is the mark God sets upon virtue... In private places, among sordid objects, an act of truth or heroism seems at once to draw to itself the sky as its temple, the sun as its candle... A virtuous man is in unison with her works..."[79]

And *there* we find the ultimate intention of Nature, of the divine Creation.

While experiencing Nature, our souls become uncluttered from the artificial, noisy, and corrupting influences of the world. As we cultivate our "eyes to see, and ears to hear," this divine music will sink deep into our souls and will enlighten and purify our mind to better distinguish and discern Truth.

"DISTRACTIONS"

By Thomas Carter

The Earth whispered softly in my ear (softly so that I could hear),

"You are my son, We are Life in each other."

    But I was cold and wet, and reached for my raincoat and

        mittens.

    I did not feel the warmth of the Earth;

    I felt the comfort of my artificed shelter

    And the rustle of my clothing muffled the whisper of the

        Earth.

The Grass fragranced sweet and savory (pungent so that I could feel),

"Our life is one, we know each other."

    But I was late for school, and tramped the grass beneath my

        feet.

    I did not feel the life in the Grass;

    I felt my solid new leather shoes snug on my feet

    And the color of my bright new lunchbox stifled the

        fragrance of the Grass.

The Blue Sky spoke deep to my soul (peacefully so that I could see),

"Lift up your gaze, and behold Life in the Heavens."

    But I supposed a check was in the mail, and rushed to the

        mailbox to pick it up.

    I only glanced at the expanse of the Heavens;

    I caressed the crisp paper check in my fingers

    And the visions of a new toy truck eclipsed the landscape of

        the Sky.

The Trees called softly in my ear (softly in the breeze so that I could hear),
"Behold the stature of a man, straight and tall, strong, honest and true."
    But I had dropped my pocket watch, and fumbled to the
        ground to find it.
    I did not see the stature of a man drawn up before me;
    I peeked at the timepiece and hurried off to dinner
    And my plate of meat and potatoes absorbed my hunger for
        truth.
The wild Thunder rumbled directly in my ear (rumbled mightily so that I could hear),
"The God of Nature is powerful to Save!"
    But I hid in the basement, clasped my hands to my ears, and
        would not hear.
    I did not hear His voice magnificent in the storm;
    I cowered in the darkness for the storm to pass
    And complained of the noise and the wind, and I would not
        hear.
The Creation speaks its languages to our senses (speaks clearly, iridescently, and purely, so that we may see and hear)
"There is a God, who moves to Save mankind, make him Heir of Life in all its majesty and glory!"
    But we prefer our own fickle imaginations, wants, and
        ambitions.
    We busy ourselves with petty diversions;
    We catch a glimpse, and feel inspired enough to purchase a
        poster, photo, or cheap imitation
    And the distractions of our ordinary lives darken the
        luminous light and revelation
    Of who we really are.

12

Truth and Religion

The essence of truth is divine

"Ye Shall Know the Truth, and the Truth Shall Make You Free"

-- John 8:32

"It is the fashion, nowadays, to dismiss God from life altogether and insist on the possibility of reaching the highest kind of life without the necessity of a living faith in a living God. I must confess my inability to drive the truth of the law home to those who have no faith in, and no need for, a power infinitely higher than themselves. My own experience has led me to the knowledge that fullest life is impossible without an immovable belief in a living law, in obedience to which the whole universe moves. A man without that faith is like a drop thrown out of the ocean which is bound to perish."[80] --Gandhi

The Bible states, "The fool hath said in his heart, 'There is no God,'" (Psalm 53:1). God has commanded men to believe in Him. This act of believing in God is a choice. This act requires faith, and the step-by-step process of choosing to believe, acting on that choice by obedience to His commandments, and listening to the "still small voice" within each person that confirms the truth. Martin Luther King, Jr. counseled, "Take the first step in faith. You don't have to see the whole staircase, just take the first step." This process develops understanding and culminates with knowledge. It is a sure and safe path to truth.

There are many who profess to teach the truth about God. But, perhaps in no other aspect of truth is it more critical to know that the truth about God does not come from man, but by revelation from God, Himself. Is it so incredulous to believe that the God of the universe would not be able, or willing, to reveal His presence to mankind? Thus, the knowledge of God will not come from philosophical or academic reasoning, university degrees, or the study of ancient manuscripts, or even the consensus of tradition or public opinion.

The truth about God comes by direct revelation: to His prophets, who then testify of him to the people, and to individuals through his Spirit or the Holy Ghost. His religion, or his Kingdom on earth, is based on continuous revelation to his prophets. Through these authorized servants the powers of redemption and the ordinances of salvation are administered to men. Individuals may receive revelation through the Holy Ghost for themselves, of the truth of what the prophets say. Individuals also may receive revelation directly from God through His Spirit and the Holy Ghost pertaining to their own personal lives. The Spirit of God will enlighten all those who seek the truth with faith, and are willing to follow their God-given conscience to obey his commandments. This knowledge of truth is beyond the factual evidence of the senses, and is a spiritual gift, discerned only spiritually—it transcends the senses. It is the surest guide to what is true. As one chooses to listen to the prophets and learns to hear this still small voice that is the manifestation of God to his soul, he experiences truth in its most pure and certain form.

The most important truths of life are learned in this way.

"I am convinced that there is no simple formula or technique that I could give you that would immediately facilitate your mastering the ability to be guided by the Holy Spirit. Our Father expects you to learn how to obtain that divine help by exercising faith in Him and His Holy Son... He knows that essential personal growth will come as you struggle to learn how to be led by the Spirit. That struggle will develop your immortal character as you perfect your capacity to

identify His will in your life through the whisperings of the Holy Ghost."[81] --
Richard G. Scott

The world is in utter confusion and conflict over the great moral questions of our time, such as our identity as individuals, abortion, gay marriage, transgender issues, and sexual morality. On any given question, "motivated human reasoning" offers justification for almost any behavior. We have been unable on our own to come to a consensus on what is right, and thus, without the revelation of God, every man is left to the exigencies of his own limited perspective, experience, and opinion.

Perhaps more than ever before the revelation of God is needed to provide a sure standard or guide to human behavior. As we substitute our own wisdom for the word of God, we flounder in a sea of doubt, uncertainty, error, and confusion.

"If (we) are acquainted with the revelations, there is no question—personal or social or political or occupational—that need go unanswered... Therein we find principles of truth that resolve every confusion and every problem and every dilemma that will face the human family or any individual in it."[82] -- Boyd K. Packer

Religion vs Revelation

There is a difference between religion and revelation. Many religions, or religious sects, are not revealed religions, but are man-made, or distortions or perversions of the original, pure religion established by God. Many men and women with deep religious spirituality, avowing their firm belief in God, living a devout and righteous life, have not associated themselves with any particular religious sect, perhaps because of this very reason. They have embraced many of the fundamental values and teachings of a moral philosophy or religion, but have rejected the dogma, which they recognize as incomplete or false. This is particularly true in our day, when many have been put off by the rigid and impossible dogmas and hypocrisies of many of the modern religious sects. Sometimes this fosters discouragement and cynicism that clouds and threatens hope of finding true religion. For those who doubt the existence of true religion, this is an invitation to consider anew a fresh look at the possibilities of God's revelation to you.

I am a Christian, but I have observed that inspiration from God is not restricted to the Christian religions. Great truths have been revealed to men and women everywhere in every age and continue to be so..

How the truth makes us free

The truth delivers us from false beliefs about our identity, our origins, the purpose of our lives, and our destiny. It teaches us the essence of our relationship to each other, to God, and to the universe. As we wholly commit ourselves to the truth, we are freed from ignorance and our human prejudices, biases, and false motivations; and then we gain confidence in our ability to walk the straight and narrow path of faith. This is truly a liberating experience. Then, we are free to move forward aligned with the laws of the universe. And thus, we may obtain unto ourselves the power to participate with God in His purposes. We become an actual active force for good in the ever-expanding creation of the universe.

As we keep His commandments and believe in Christ, we experience the power of the Atonement of Jesus Christ, and are freed from our weak and carnal natures. The healing power of Jesus Christ may heal and deliver us from our pain, sorrow, or addictions. He strengthens our weakness and delivers us from our infirmities in a truly miraculous transformation that fills our hearts with gratitude, happiness and peace. In so doing, we rise to our most complete potential and full stature as sons and daughters of God. I have felt this redeeming power and know that it is real.

13

Truth and the Arts

"Poetry is that impassioned arrangement of words, whether in verse or prose, which embodies
the exaltation, the beauty, the rhythm and the truth of life."[83]
-- Richard Gallienne

There is a wealth of enjoyment, wisdom and truth found in the arts: poetry, literature, music, drama, painting, and sculpture. All great art is symbolic of eternal verities. The humanities hold a unique power to impart understanding and insight into the human condition, to lift the mind, comfort a troubled spirit, and inspire vision. I love a good book. I have read many good books that have inspired me to thoughts above and beyond my own imagination. All great literature strengthens character and teaches virtue, because it appeals to our common human nature and enlightens our minds to reality and truth.

Great music is a window into heaven. It imparts comfort, sweetness and strengthens virtue. While appealing to our most tender human feelings, it reminds us of our kinship with all that is good. How often do we find comfort and pleasure in the silent contemplation of a good book, of a great piece of art, of the soaring strains of sweet and powerful music that enlarges and expands the imagination and enlightenment of our soul? Or a poem such as this, that lifts our imagination to the contemplation of the divine.

The Voice of God

"If God speaks anywhere, in any voice,

To us his creatures, surely here and now

We hear him, while the great chords seem to bow

Our heads, and all the symphony's breathless noise

Breaks over us, with challenge to our souls!

Beethoven's music! From the mountain peaks

The strong, divine, compelling thunder rolls;

And 'Come up higher!' are the words it speaks,

'Out of your darkened valleys of despair;

Behold, I lift you up on mighty wings

Into Hope's living, reconciling air!

Breathe, and forget your life's perpetual stings,--

Dream, folded on the breast of Patience sweet;

Some pulse of pitying love for you may beat.'"

--Celia Thaxter[84]

One must use careful judgment because the arts can also be used to distract from the truth by creating a false reality, clouding vision, appealing to the carnal instincts, and can even destroy virtuous motivation. Uninspired human talent is fallible and not a trusted source for truth. One can discern what is good by listening to his heart and choosing that which is edifying, uplifting and inspiring, consistent with moral values and wise principles, and avoiding that which is trite, carnal, shallow, and degrading to the human condition. By this I do not mean to avoid literature that authentically explores the dark side of human nature. Any literature that brings understanding to human nature and the human condition is valuable and helps us to see reality more clearly.

One of the benefits of great art, literature, and music is a deeper and more profound insight and understanding of reality, and an increased confidence in knowledge of truth. A perfect example is Ralph Waldo Emerson's poem, "The Rhodora."

"THE RHODORA:

ON BEING ASKED, WHENCE IS THE FLOWER?

In May, when sea-winds pierced our solitudes,

I found the fresh Rhodora in the woods,

Spreading its leafless blooms in a damp nook,

To please the desert and the sluggish brook.

The purple petals, fallen in the pool,

Made the black water with their beauty gay;

Here might the red-bird come his plumes to cool,

And court the flower that cheapens his array.

Rhodora! if the sages ask thee why

This charm is wasted on the earth and sky,

Tell them, dear, that if eyes were made for seeing,

Then Beauty is its own excuse for being:

Why thou wert there, O rival of the rose!

I never thought to ask, I never knew;

But, in my simple ignorance, suppose

The self-same Power that brought me there brought you.

-- Ralph Waldo Emerson

14
Truth and Politics

A rich battleground of truth vs error

Confusion, power, greed and deception govern our current national politics. A trend towards a dangerous secular philosophy, the compulsion to win at all costs, and biased pride dominates. The first casualty is truth.

The politics of our generation is deteriorating in alarming ways, reminiscent of the corrupted politics of the Greek and Roman empires during their decline and destruction. The glory and strength of our democracy has always been our ability to discuss and debate in an atmosphere of freedom of speech, with an expectation that mature adults committed to what is right will usually find a consensus of what is good. Looking at the current political wars, I see this tradition in deep jeopardy. No longer, it seems, are we able to intelligently discuss and debate. We just settle in our most comfortable and advantageous position and demonize the opposition! Opposing views are being shut out and shut down, and the conversation isn't rational debate, but a mad race to exert the power to come out on top!

While only recently differing opinions and viewpoints were considered alternate paths at arriving at the same goal, now, the very goals of competing political interests differ, so that we now disagree about the fundamental values and principles that will determine what we are as a people and as a country. We see this in the polarization of the electorate between the political parties in the U.S., Republican and Democrat, and the far-right and the far-left.

"Politics has always been adversarial. Traditionally, though, we've had a fairly robust national consensus about a fairly broad set of goals—a strong defense, a decent safety net, freedom from excessive government interference—even though we've squabbled over how to achieve them. What's different about (current) politics is the transformation of even nonpartisan issues into mad-as-hell battles of the bases, which makes it virtually impossible for politicians to solve problems in a two-party system. Cooperation and compromise start to look like capitulation, or even treasonous collusion with the enemy."[85]

Instead of what is right and what is wrong, we are obsessed with who is right, and who is wrong. Instead of finding common ground upon which to agree and move forward, accusation and demonization of the other party is the new norm.

The traditional American values of Liberty, belief in God, E pluribus Unum (out of many, one), truth, and virtue are under direct frontal assault as never before. The time-honored expedient of disagreeing with our neighbor with respect and patience has now evolved into "hate thy neighbor" and "silence him" if he disagrees with you. In this setting, it has become difficult to even to talk about politics with someone who disagrees. Incivility, intolerance, and even violence are increasingly common on our national political scene. We have seen this in the increasingly frequent episodes of violent demonstration in the U.S. by the Antifa movement as well as the far-right white supremacists.

In this context we are inundated by passionate arguments and obfuscations, promoted by "talking heads" and "experts" of every persuasion, trying to manipulate our emotions and influence our views. The dizzying talking points of each interest group complicate and confuse, rather than clarify. In this morass of opinion and argument, it's not easy to remain clear-headed and objective.

This breeds cynicism, disillusionment, and discouragement. Perhaps we find the easiest course is to simply comfort ourselves by accepting what matches our natural emotion or self-interest. What is easy for me to believe? What do I want to believe?

Surely, we can find rational explanation that will support what we want to believe, and that is the work of every politician: to give the people a reason to believe what they want to believe. We can even "cherry pick" the facts that we want to hear. We then choose the narrative that matches our comfort zone and favors the evidence that supports our preferred view. Eventually, we choose to believe just what we want to believe. We fool ourselves with a false certainty that our opinion has to be the right one. "If one attitude characterizes modern politics, it's an attitude of complete and utter moral certainty." -- Ben Shapiro[86] Or, we just stick our heads in the sand and pretend that we don't care, and that our opinion doesn't matter.

As we choose to believe what we want to believe, which can be an illusion of truth, we lose sight of what is real, and we lose our integrity. This is a recipe for division and polarization, as each side moves farther and farther from the other. First, we disagree (at least we are still talking). Then we demonize (now we are not talking). Then we hate (now we are silencing the other side). Then we have lost the ability to collaborate and work together. This is surely the path that will destroy us as a people and as a Nation.

In the heat of the political battle, we must find a way to cast off our divisive conversation, misunderstood motives, selfish interests, and look to reliable standards of truth. Otherwise, we will be lost in the seas of controversy and contention. As mature adults, surely we should be able to find common ground to advance liberty and freedom and the special American values that so many have given their lives for. This is possible to the extent that we are really committed to truth and are willing to give up our egocentric personal interests in favor of what is right.

I believe this. And it may easier than you think. It lies in emphasizing our common values of morality, decency, and fairness, and in identifying simple core principles. It lies in an individual search and commitment to what is true. It lies in giving up the illusion of knowing truth and reclaiming our integrity by identifying and honoring what is actually true.

A Plea for the Triumph of Principles

Principles trump expediency. A firm reliance on sound, time-tested principles will guide us through the muddied waters of expediency and land us on the shore of certainty. It takes faith to rely on principle rather than expediency.

Here are several principles that will help us to find clarity and unity:

Objectivity--a commitment to the truth above all else is the crucial starting point. Objectivity is an appeal to develop a consistent method of testing information—a transparent approach to evidence—precisely so that personal and cultural biases do not undermine the accuracy...[87]   What is the primary commitment of any particular argument? Is it to a party, to an ideology, to money interests, to personal interests? Is it to a weaving secular philosophy? What is the standard for its credibility? Does it subscribe to a malleable relativistic interpretation of reality, or does it lie solid on the firm foundation of established values and principles?

Belief in God: Our prosperity and success as a people and as a Nation is absolutely dependent upon our belief in God and our willingness to obey His commandments. We may safely conclude that any idea, philosophy, policy, or act that leads away from this core principle is detrimental to our liberty and prosperity, and to the cause of truth.

The arc of the universe: There is a fundamental imperative that is at the root of all human action. It is this: In the conflicting interests and complex interactions of our politics, reality will have its sway. Legitimate and authentic interests will hold their own, and, though falsity, deception, and fraud will attempt to dominate and control, only the true interests of right will predominate in the long run. This is the arc of the universe and should give us great confidence and assurance that good will eventually prevail.

"Things have their laws, as well as men; and things refuse to be trifled with...Under any forms, persons and property must and will have their just sway... the attributes of a person, his will and his moral energy, will exercise, under any law or extinguishing tyranny, their proper force, if not overtly, then covertly; if not for the law, then against it; if not wholesomely, then poisonously; with right, or by might.

"We are not at the mercy of any waves of chance. In the strife of ferocious parties, human nature always finds itself cherished;

"No forms can have any dangerous importance whilst we are befriended by the laws of things... Absolute right is the first governor."[88] --Ralph Waldo Emerson, "Politics"

All things work together for the good of those who act consistent with the laws of the universe.[89]

Defend the Constitution. We need to believe and trust in the Declaration of Independence and the Constitution as inspired documents. They set forth the fundamental principles of freedom and liberty and divided government that make America great, and they must be defended and preserved by freedom-loving men and women. I believe that they are a bulwark and a defense against tyranny and anarchy.

Become Informed. "The only thing necessary for the triumph of evil is that good men should do nothing," stated the English scholar, Edmund Burke.

It's important to be informed as to the basic facts and all the sides of any issue. One must know the opposing arguments to any particular controversy and the options for solutions to be able to compete in the private or public debate. It's vital to know your opponent so you know what you are up against. Then you can more effectively combat untruths, obfuscations and diversions.

Listen to your adversary and be open to accept and embrace whatever elements of truth that he holds. By so doing, you will enhance your credibility as a sincere seeker of truth, and empower him, and others, to listen and collaborate with you. Plutarch, the wise and reputable historian of Roman times, stated,

> "... we must give to everyone his due, to an enemy such respect and honor as he truly deserves. Thus a man that praises his enemy for his real deserts shall himself obtain the more honor by it; and whenever he shall correct or censure him, he will be credited in what he does, because everyone will believe that he does it out of a dislike and just abhorrence of his vice and not of his person."[90]

You will also learn of the weakness of your own position, and gain valuable knowledge and insight to improve and enhance your own understanding of the truth.

Sometimes your most committed enemy may actually be your best benefactor. His accusation of your weakness can be a valuable source of insight.

> "... the wise and prudent make good use of the hatred and enmity of men...
>
> "... we (should) be circumspect and wary in everything we speak or do, as if our enemy always stood at our elbow and overlooked every action. Hence, we learn to lead blameless and inoffensive lives...
>
> "... Plato, when he was in company with any persons that were guilty of unhandsome actions, was wont thus to reflect upon himself and ask this question, 'Am I of the like temper and disposition with these men?' In like manner, whosoever passes a hard censure upon another man's life should presently make use of self-examination and enquire what his own is; by which means he will come to know what his failings are, and how to amend them. Thus the very censures and backbitings of his enemy will redound to his advantage...
>
> "Whenever then anything is spoken against you that is not true, do not pass it by or despise it because it is false, but forthwith examine yourself, and consider what you have said or done, what you have ever undertaken, or what converse you have ever had that may have given likelihood to the slander...
>
> "... why should not we take an enemy for our tutor, who will instruct us gratis in those things we knew not before?[91]

Nothing good is free and we cannot expect the high road to be the easy road. A man must diligently seek the truth, and pay the price to become informed and wise. As we are disinterested bystanders, whether from discouragement, cynicism, or laziness, we risk losing our liberty to the forces of ignorance, discord and tyranny. Can we expect to enjoy the blessings of liberty that others have sacrificed their lives for if we are not willing to make our own sacrifice to become virtuous, informed and involved citizens?

Freedom for the Individual, Agency and Accountability are crucial principles that are important principles to remember. There is a pernicious attitude and philosophy abroad that seeks to nullify the agency of man. In the claimed interest of the greater good, this philosophy seeks to coerce persons into doing the right thing. It seeks to manipulate and force individuals into acting in conformity to the established mantra. It is a recipe for tyranny. [92]

Are we trying to improve society by changing men's hearts by teaching them virtue and correct principles, or are we trying to coerce them? It's much easier to force people to do good than to successfully teach them to do good. Man has agency given to act for himself. Measures to manipulate, coerce, or force in the interest of a greater good vitiate liberty and one's freedom to act. It seems that as a society, we have almost forgotten how to encourage good behavior by teaching virtue, and instead have resorted to coercion at every level to make people do the right thing. This practice teaches us to not think for ourselves, and is shaping us into pawns and slaves, eventually ripe for oppression.

"Freedom to order our own conduct in the sphere where material circumstances force a choice upon us, and responsibility for the arrangement of our own life according to our own conscience, is the air in which alone moral sense grows and in which moral values are daily re-created in the free decision of the individual. Responsibility, not to a superior, but to one's conscience, the awareness of a duty not exacted by compulsion, the necessity to decide which of the things one values are to be sacrificed to others, and to bear the consequences of one's own decision, are the very essence of any morals which deserve the name... A movement whose main promise is the relief from responsibility cannot but be antimoral in its effect..."[93] (--John Stuart Mill)

Honesty is the best policy is a gold standard. As a basic principle of politics, honesty is always to be insisted upon. When we see dishonest communication and underhanded tactics, one must suspect the soundness of the underlying interest. Virtue and right will stand on their own merits without resorting to dishonesty and unauthentic contrivance.

Recognize and cease to tolerate corruption. I feel so strongly about this. Many are participating in willful corruption and deception. This needs to be recognized for what it is. Corruption and lies can be fought by standing for truth and speaking up courageously when appropriate. Taking a stand for truth requires courage. However, we must ever remember in our standing for truth to be kind and tolerant, as well as firm. When one feels passionate, it can sometimes come across as self-righteousness. I myself have been guilty of this, forgetting that "it's more important to be loving than to be right". Promoting veracity and virtue in one's personal life is essential, but one must avoid dogmatism and self-righteousness. There is no greater turn-off than the obsequious holier-than-thou self-righteousness from one who portrays himself alone as the judge of others. We are all human and have potential for evil and are vulnerable to deception. This should make us humble and nonjudgmental of others. But one must have no part in illegal or dishonest activities, avoiding even the appearance of corruption.

Sometimes it will not be possible to compromise or collaborate when fundamental differences of values and principles exist. Then, one must stand courageously and unequivocally for what one believes is right. He can do that when he confidently places his beliefs on reliable standards of truth.

A measure of a man's patriotism indeed may be the extent to which he will choose to find and believe the truth and then act upon it in the interest of his country. This is dependent upon his integrity and virtue and commitment to what is right.

WHAT IF WE CAN'T AGREE ON THESE PRINCIPLES?

Then go to a more fundamental, human position, and apply more basic and fundamental principles of humanity, such as:

"Do unto others as you would have them do unto you."[94] Love and respect for others is the most powerful tool we have to influence each other for good, and to achieve common agreement and purpose. When we demonize others, we lose the ability to influence them. Those that seek to tear down others with destructive criticism and hateful speech create an atmosphere of contention and division, destroying any possibility of mutual understanding and unity.

To constructively criticize or disagree leads to the possibility of rational thought and collaboration. Indeed, as we respectfully listen and engage with those with differing viewpoints, we may be able to achieve mutual understanding and agreement. Compromise may be enabled, and unity of purpose becomes possible.

Teach your children and family correct principles and use your influence for good in your own social circles as much as you can. The ripple effect of these efforts, magnified and exponentially repeated, has the potential to change the world.

Virtue triumphs. Do what is right. The bedrock principle of all successful human interaction is virtue. As we practice honesty and integrity in all aspects of our lives, our example will be above reproach, and we can operate from a position of moral authority. It won't make us superior or better than others, but it will place us in an exemplary position to inspire others to their best behavior, enhance our own credibility, and create an atmosphere where cooperation and unity is possible.

Mixing it up—Competing Principles

Sound principles may appear to compete with each other, such as justice and mercy. Careful consideration is required to reveal the predominant principle that is active and relevant. The best political choice is often a mixture of good and bad, truth and error, but will contain the most central or predominant proportion of truth. Human affairs are complicated, and rarely does truth manifest itself through imperfect humans in a pure form. Even execution of sound policy based on truth will often be flawed because of the imperfections of the instrument—those intrinsically flawed human actors represented by each one of us.

The worst choice will also incorporate a mixture of truth and error. The most misguided and perverted philosophies and beliefs will have elements of truth.

The mature and sincere seeker for truth will apply reliable standards to assess political or moral positions. Careful and thorough inquiry, application of God-given values, and sound, time-tested principles, together with confidence in one's inner voice of common sense and revelation, will lead the committed seeker to an understanding of wisdom and truth. One must inform himself and carefully consider options. He must apply wisdom, and all means at his disposal to discern sound policy and truth. He must pay the price. Then, when he is confident that he has found truth, he can share it and defend it, not from personal interest or bias, but from the sure, unassailable position of knowledge of things as they really are.

A Call to Action

How will we as a people ever attain to the state where we look to our common values, principles, and to God for wisdom, so we have a semblance of unity of understanding and purpose?

The answer to this question does not lie in the halls of power at the seat of our government. It lies in the collective behavior and influence of each person, and in his commitment to virtue and truth. "If we have any hope of reclaiming the good will and sense of humanity for which we yearn, it must begin with each of us, one person at a time," stated President Russell M Nelson, President of the Church of Jesus Christ of Latter-Day Saints.95

It must start with each individual—with each one of us. Then, it spreads to our families and our friends, and then to our associates. It is said that each individual knows about 1000 persons. If each one of us could influence for good these 1000 persons, and each one of those could then influence another 1000 persons, soon the whole world will be changed!

But this needs to be more than an ordinary conversion and endeavor that languishes in our conflicted motives and commitments. It will require an assertive, enthusiastic, and mighty movement that will capture the imagination and commitment of the whole world. It may take time to develop. It will take an epic leader to galvanize action in a great forward movement.

But it can start now—with you and me, as we seek out truth, believe it, embrace it, and then share and defend it within the circles of our own influence, however great or small. This personal commitment will grow and expand until it becomes a mighty force for good. Then we will find the power to unify our purpose and act together for the betterment of humanity.

At some point, we can only hope and pray that the truth in politics will merge with the truths of science, of the humanities, of religion, and will gather into one universal understanding of the reality of all things as they really are.

15

Truth and Bias

the universal Achilles' heel

In previous chapters, we have discussed how bias may impede one's ability to discern truth. This is such a universal problem that I have felt it necessary to deal with it in its own chapter.

I struggle with this issue every day, as I realize that the sincere and committed seeker of truth must carefully analyze his opinions and beliefs to remove unwarranted or untrue biases.

Overcoming our own bias is a fairly rigorous and difficult task for everyone. But, as we recognize that our biases are artificial narratives, then hopefully we can find the insight and power to give them up in favor of truth.

Often, our biases are not obvious to us. They seem to be spontaneous and natural, and often color our thinking, opinions, and beliefs with us scarcely being aware. They are very powerful determinants of our perception of truth.

How do we identify and give up our biases? Let's break this down: In order to give up our biases, we must first identify them, and then judge their validity.

A simple exercise may help one to identify his/her biases and their validity:

- For a particular controversy, identify your relevant core values and basic principles. Identify competing values and principles and prioritize them.
- For a particular issue, look within and state your most natural and ready opinion or belief, or the one that you want to be true. This is probably your bias.

- Ask yourself why you have that opinion or belief.

- Ask yourself on what your opinion or belief is based upon. (review in chapter 4 the reasons people believe the way they do.)

- Is the opinion based on a fair review of the facts? Are you adequately informed on the issue at hand, so you know the pertinent facts?

- Is the opinion based on sound values and principles? (It may be helpful to identify the particular values and principles underlying your opinion or belief)

- Is the opinion based on or consistent with known revelation?

- Are there any ulterior motives that are directing your opinion or belief, such as monetary gain, personal prejudice, lifestyle choice, etc.? (review Chapter 6, "false standards and impediments to truth")

- Answer the question: "Is my bias on this issue valid, and consistent with the truth?"

- Ask yourself, "Am I willing to give up my bias if it is not consistent with the truth?

Remember, an identified bias is your choice to believe, and it is your privilege and responsibility to use your agency in either holding on to it and strengthening it, or giving it up in favor of the truth, if necessary.

Here are some examples that I have identified from some of my own past thinking:

EXAMPLE #1

A common belief I hear is that "All politicians are corrupt." Is this true?

1. My core values include honesty, trustworthiness, and loyalty.

A basic principle that I believe in is that a public servant is there to serve the public's interest as best he can and resist corrupting influences.

2. My most ready opinion is that all politicians are corrupt. This may be my bias.

3. I carry that belief because I see corruption and dishonesty and self-interest everywhere in the political arena. Politicians act just to get power and to get re-elected.

4. This opinion is based on my impression from watching the news occasionally and hearing people talk. My Dad always said that all politicians are corrupt.

- I don't watch the news regularly because I hate the way politicians talk about each other. Also, it is so confusing that I don't know who is telling the truth or has the right answer. So, I haven't really become informed on all of the politicians. I just know that the ones that I hear seem to be corrupt.

- The only revelation that I am aware of on this subject is that my religious leaders have said we should be informed and elect honest and reliable representatives.

- It does serve my self-interest, however, because if all politicians are corrupt, that relieves me of a vast burden in taking political sides and figuring out who is right. I can just sit back and point fingers.

5. On closer thought, maybe it's not fair to say that all politicians are corrupt. I know that some are. Come to think of it, I do know of one politician that I trust and admire because he takes honest positions sometimes that I respect. So, my bias that all politicians are corrupt doesn't seem to be supported by the facts. In fact, as I think about it more, maybe there are more than I know that are honest. I need to inform myself more thoroughly.

6. Yes, I will give up my bias against politicians.

7. I will become more informed and engaged in the political process and not use this general stereotype to judge politicians. By doing this, I could be part of the answer, rather than part of the problem.

EXAMPLE #2:

"People who don't go to church are bad people."

1. My core value is of obedience to God's commandments. That includes honesty, kindness, loving your neighbor, sexual purity, and loving God.

The basic principle that I ascribe to is that by going to church, I learn about God and am strengthened in keeping His commandments.

I guess a competing value is not to be judgmental of others. But I have to judge others in order to be clear on the importance of keeping the commandments.

2. My most ready opinion is that if people don't go to church, they don't care about keeping God's commandments. I really want to believe that. This must be my bias.

3. I believe that because that is what my parents said, and I have always thought that. It's a simple explanation of why people are bad.

4. This opinion is based on the fact that most people in jail don't go to church, and they are bad people.

     - But, when I think about it, I remember a member of our congregation who went to jail for stealing money from his company. I wonder how many people who go to church really go to jail. I'm sure that some do. Also, I know a person who goes to church every Sunday but won't speak to me because he doesn't like me. Actually, a friend told me that this man beats his wife at home. I'm not sure if the facts really support my belief on this. And, actually, one of my best friends, who is really a good man, doesn't go to church.

     - God said to love your neighbor, and to "judge not, that ye be not judged." He also said that the Pharisees were hypocrites because they made a great show of going to church but were hateful and unkind to their neighbors.

     - To be honest, by thinking that other people are bad just because they don't go to church, it makes me look good because I always go to church.

5. I don't think it's fair to say that people are bad because they don't go to church. This is a bias that I have that is not true. It would be true to say that some people who don't go to church are bad; but also, that some people who go to church are bad, too.

6. It will be kind of hard to give up this bias, because I have believed it for a long time. But yes, I will choose to give it up.

7. I will be less judgmental of others.

To really slay this monster of bias in my own thinking, I have found it necessary to constantly remind myself of my vulnerability to it, test my thinking frequently and carefully against reliable standards, and to consciously be willing to rid myself of it, to let it go. Just the conscious decision to let go of my identified biases, I have found, is very powerful. I must say, honestly, though, that I remain vulnerable to bias, and that I have to continually strive in putting forth my best efforts to combat it.

16

Truth and Science

the great dichotomy: the tangible vs the spiritual

There seems to be an ongoing conflict between Science and Religion, which when reduced to its simplest terms, is actually a conflict between the tangible (sensory-based), expressed in scientific terms, and the spiritual, reflected in the necessity of revelation for a fullness of truth. Can they be reconciled? Of course, when one considers the essential elements of both views, and is honest about the limitations, and peculiar advantages of each. Used together, they offer a reliable path towards truth.

Science is man's effort to discover truths about the physical universe. Modern scientists employ the Scientific Method. The Oxford English Dictionary defines the scientific method as "a method or procedure that has characterized natural science since the 17th century, consisting in systematic observation, measurement, and experiment, and the formulation, testing, and modification of hypotheses."

The explosion of scientific and technological knowledge that has resulted in the stunning advancements of understanding of our world can be attributed to the usefulness of this method. Advancements in technology of physics, computer science, communication, data management, astronomy, industry, agriculture, and medicine, to mention only a few, have transformed man's ability to control his environment and produce a way of life and standard of living never before seen on the earth. So much of our understanding of the world we live in can be credited to the systematic use of the scientific method. We have learned to harness the miracles of electricity, of communication and transportation in the digital world that we live in—all to the production of a truly advanced technological culture.

Thus, the scientific method has generally proven to be a reliable source of truth within the sphere of the material, or physical universe accessible to our observation.

Yet, the method has limitations. The problem with the scientific method is that our powers of observation are limited to the human senses within our own time and space. Even with the most sophisticated scientific technology, observations by direct or indirect evidence are still limited by our powers of sight, hearing, and touch. We are unable to observe many of the basic and fundamental facts of the universe. The elemental nature of matter, energy, motion, and light remain to be illuminated. Dark matter, dark energy, space and time, remain to be fully understood. The existence of God, his omnipresence and power, spiritual identity and manifestations, the existence of supernatural beings, life, and death have yet to be fully explained by science. However, we know that these things exist. We simply do not have access to observe all of the fundamental facts that explain some of these truths that we do know exist. The "God particle" has yet to be found.

Modern scientific theory, known as the "Principle of Uncertainty" further illustrates the limitations of science in describing truth. Jacob Bronowski, in *The Ascent of Man*, explains, "One aim of the physical sciences has been to give an exact picture of the material world. One achievement of physics in the twentieth century has been to prove that that aim is unattainable."[96]

As scientific research continues to add information about the physical world, the picture is never quite complete. As our powers of observation increase in detail, the images improve, but are always curtailed by the limits of our physical senses. He further states,

> "The perfect image is still as remote as the distant stars... "We are here face to face with the crucial paradox of knowledge. Year by year we devise more precise instruments with which to observe nature with more fineness. And

when we look at the observations, we are discomfited to see that they are still fuzzy, and we feel that they are as uncertain as ever. We seem to be running after a goal which lurches away from us to infinity every time we come within sight of it...

"We had hoped that the human errors would disappear, and that we would ourselves have God's view. But it turns out that the errors cannot be taken out of the observations.... we discover that there is no God's eye view. The errors are inextricably bound up with the nature of human knowledge...

"... whatever the fundamental units the world is put together from, they are more delicate, more fugitive, more startling than we catch in the butterfly net of our senses."[97]

Another source for error stems from the basic assumption of modern-day research and science that fundamental processes of the universe operate uniformly throughout the universe at all times and places (uniformitarianism). This is a basic assumption of the scientific method. Many scientists also presume that the universe was created and has evolved without the intervention of a superior power (naturalism). "Though science has conceded an infinite number of possible viewpoints for describing any object, in practice it has always insisted that there is really only one valid viewpoint: the down-to-earth, no-nonsense reality of everyday experience. We see everything, as it were, through a long, thin tube set up at an immovable point and welded in position to face in one direction only. What do we know of reality?"[98]

These assumptions or presumptions are not necessarily valid. Of course, one cannot know for a certainty whether or not the conditions at the beginning of the world are the same as today. One cannot go back and observe physical processes at the origin of the universe. Therefore, we have made assumptions necessary to our rational investigation. We have observed a paucity of facts and have, through inductive reasoning, proposed scientific theories that appear to be consistent in explaining many phenomena. We have taken relatively few facts from incomplete observations of matter and motion on the earth of our own time, and even fewer facts from observation of the heavens, and have extrapolated these to apply to the whole universe throughout all time. This is an incomplete picture at best, and a fundamental false premise and miscalculation at worst.

Our understanding of the universe continues to expand with new facts and knowledge. Thus, science is an evolving, and necessarily unfinished, source of truth that is dependent upon limited observations in time and space. (We may catch a glimpse of the difficulty when we consider what we are learning about space and time, that they may be elastic, and what we understand as time, may not be a finite property of matter.)

Yes, to the extent that the underlying assumptions are true, much scientific progress has been made and many truths discovered. However, it would be foolish to contain all truth to what the scientific method can discover, for that method is a very temporal process adapted to our present physical world and based on our own limited and fallible observations.

We must therefore conclude that science is an imperfect tool for finding truth. It is useful in illuminating the physical properties of our current world and has added much knowledge that has been harnessed for the advancement and refinement of our technology and standard of living.

And yet, when science is inspired by the divine, marvelous verities and realities are discovered. Socrates, Plato, and Newton all relate how they were converted, "not away from the study of physical science, but to seeing in physical science ... the workings of a divine and directing mind."[99] "Descartes, with purely scientific interest in view, believed that his world-shaking discovery in mathematics was given to him in visions."[100] Some modern-day scientists also believe in the spiritual: "Yes, the triumphs of the physical scientists are impressive enough to explain why science has a great reputation... But the mysteries of life—perhaps they are intended to remain mysteries."[101] "The inductive format of the scientific paper should be discarded, ... and scientists should not be ashamed, ... as many of them apparently are ashamed to admit, that hypotheses... are imaginative and inspirational in character... They are indeed adventures of the mind."[102]

"Hypotheses arise by guesswork. That is to put it in its crudest form. I should say rather that they arise by inspiration."[103] "The most beautiful thing we can experience is the mysterious."[104]

The very nature of the scientific method limits its usefulness and reliability in answering the most important, existential, questions of life, such as "Who are we? Where did we come from? What is our destiny?

The curse of science is when it is used to explain the universe without God (naturalism).

But surely, as we put forth our best efforts in seeking truth through science, as we recognize the divine source of all truth and knowledge, and open our minds to inspiration from the Creator, and acknowledge His hand in all things, we will discover marvelous and exciting truths about the physical universe. And this is at it should be.

Truth, Science, and Medicine

As a physician, I have confidence in the medical community at large, and in the scientific method that supports evidence-based medicine. I rely on the integrity of scientific journals and the standards of medical care established from accumulated and documented experience reflected in our health care system.

Astonishing strides have been made also in the field of medicine using the scientific method and this has resulted in knowledge and technology that seems truly miraculous in our day. Current "evidence-based" medicine provides reliable treatment for myriads of health-related issues and diseases, that were never approached in a rational way before.

However, one of the most confusing arenas of reason and truth lies in the realm of "alternative medicine." Perhaps in no other area are people more vulnerable to deception and fraud. Billions of dollars are spent every year in the promotion of health products that have limited, if any, actual real positive impact on health or disease, but which carry the promise of better health or relief from pain. Because of the intensely personal nature of health and disease, individuals are keenly invested in whatever might help them feel better. Fear and hope are powerful motivators, and the purveyors of health products are well aware of this dynamic. There is much false and conflicting information available to the public that can leave the most careful consumer confused. Unscrupulous marketers of questionable products exploit and prey upon the hopes and fears of vulnerable individuals.

The placebo effect

The power of the human mind to believe what it wants is truly amazing. Even to the extent of actually causing positive results. Nowhere is this more evident than the mind's ability to grasp hoped-for, or perceived benefit as reality, or truth. Thus, millions of persons every day succumb to the lies and distortions that abound in the health services industry, in a vain hope of cure and recovery.

"The placebo effect, also known as non-specific effects and the subject-expectancy effect, is the phenomenon that a patient's symptoms can be alleviated by an otherwise ineffective treatment, since the individual expects or believes that it will work."[105]

Conversely, the "nocebo effect" is the phenomenon that a patient's symptoms may not improve if he does not expect or believe that it will work.

"Your mind can be a powerful healing tool when given the chance. The idea that your brain can convince your body a fake treatment is the real thing... and thus stimulate healing has been around for millennia. Now science has found that under the right circumstances, a placebo can be just as effective as traditional treatments.

"The placebo effect is more than positive thinking – believing a treatment or procedure will work. It's about creating a stronger connection between the brain and body and how they work together,' says Professor Ted Kaptchuk of Harvard-affiliated Beth Israel Deaconess Medical Center...

"Placebos won't lower your cholesterol or shrink a tumor. Instead, they work on symptoms modulated by the brain, like the perception of pain. 'Placebos may make you feel better, but they will not cure you,' says Kaptchuk. 'They have been shown to be most effective for conditions like pain management, stress-related insomnia, and cancer treatment side effects like fatigue and nausea.'"[106]

So often, however, fake treatments are advertised and marketed for various health benefits that are not scientifically supported, or evidence based. Myriads of products, from dietary supplements, protein or energy supplements, health remedies, and naturopathic cures are available with various claims for disease management or for healthy living. To the layperson, such claims may seem very compelling, and cultivate a hope for a cure or for feeling better. It's hard to argue that a perceived benefit to a particular individual is not real, but when extended as reality to a generalized and universal cure, without evidence which is scientifically proven, this is inaccurate at best, and deceptive at worst.

Each of us may be vulnerable to these deceptions.

Many years ago, as a freshman university student, I wrote a research paper entitled, "A Quack is Unique." It described the age-old phenomenon of quackery in medicine, and how to recognize fake, or quack, cures.

Although some of these signs are not presently relevant due to changed communication and cultural norms since then, the basic distinctions of "placebo-based," or "quackery" medicine remain the same. I have found these characteristics reliably indicative of "placebo-based" health care claims:

Is the proposed remedy promoted within the mainstream of the licensed and regulated health care community? Does the traditional medical community accept as efficacious the proposed product or cure?

One can usually be confident that our modern medical community uses evidence-based treatments consistent with the scientific method. A popular mantra is that doctors are prejudiced or biased against a certain remedy because it works too well, or they have been bought-off by "Big Pharma." This is a diversion and doesn't really make sense. Most practitioners, and the medical profession at large, have a powerful self-interest in using remedies that actually work. Of course, doctors can be biased, too, and we find many practitioners using remedies that fall into the realm of quack medicine, rather than evidence-based medicine.

Evidence-based medicine is backed up by reliable and credible scientific studies. These studies are double-blinded and employ standard statistical data analysis. Often the placebo-based or quack practitioners display their own "studies", which when closely examined, are actually pseudo-scientific. They appear to be reliable to the lay populace but do not adhere to the standards of an actual scientific study that could be published in a credible scientific journal, subject to peer review and professional scrutiny.

The use of testimonials is a common but unreliable practice. Testimonials of an individual person may be interesting, but they are not indicators of reliable, reproducible efficacy of any particular treatment. They are subject to feelings, emotion, and subjective perceptions and expectations, i.e. the "placebo effect". They do not have the benefit of a controlled setting that can isolate the determinative factor from other factors that may influence the outcome.

It is very possible that a person may actually feel better due to the powerful "placebo effect," and if she is content with that, so much the better (as long as it doesn't prevent her from seeking treatment that actually works, or gives her a false hope—or depletes her financial resources). It's a different matter, however, to promise that it will work for everybody. And that is what a scientific study attempts to settle: Is this a remedy that will consistently be effective for most people?

Does the rationale or explanation of efficacy fit into known scientific observation? Does it make sense knowing what we do know about how things work? Or does it offer a new and fantastic explanation that is not consistent with known scientific processes?

The essence of the scientific method is to be open to new knowledge that improves our understanding. But integrity demands that as we propose new theories of the nature of things, we substantiate and verify with reliable data.

Vague, rather than specific, claims of efficacy should cause suspicion. Exciting, flamboyant, and exaggerated claims that seem too good to be true usually are too good to be true. Vague claims that a product "supports" specific aspects of good health should be viewed with skepticism.

Established, reliable, and trusted sources are vital. Claims made by those who stand to profit should be suspect. Current scientific journals usually separate reliable scientific research from interests that will profit, or, they, at least, identify potential conflicts of interest.

Common sense, while seemingly in short supply these days, provides a powerful indicator of truth. In these matters, listen for the "ring of truth," and avoid fantastic and facile solutions. If It's too good to be true, it probably is too good to be true. Be aware of your emotions and bias, and determine to carefully gauge your hopes and fears, while using your best judgment to make wise decisions.

The search for truth in science and health matters is the same as in any other realm: consider the facts, reference basic values and principles, counsel the applicable revelatory history, including one's own "inner voice," or personal revelation. When proposed scientific hypotheses, or theories, conflict with established revelatory truth, one must be skeptical, and then carefully apply these sound standards to the analysis.

17

Strategies for Finding and Testing Truth

Often in the complicated and confusing world in which we live, there seems to be no clear pathway of finding truth, other than the hodge-podge of ideas, philosophies, and agendas constantly being presented to us. And it's difficult to analyze our opinions and beliefs and even know how we got them, much less to figure out if they are true or not. It might be helpful to break this whole process down into simple elements, so here is a list of simple strategies that may be helpful:

Do you have a sincere desire and firm commitment to open your soul to truth?

Are you informed and listening to both sides? Are you open to see things differently or from another's perspective? It's important to collect as much information as possible and to obtain it from trusted sources. Persevere until you understand the issue.

Can you isolate the facts, and separate them from the nonessential information and the propaganda? Then it will be easier to identify pertinent values and applicable basic principles.

It takes a focused effort to recognize the motives for your belief. What do you want to believe? Can you identify your own agenda, bias, emotions, prejudices, and preconceived notions and any other false standards for your belief?

Listen and trust your inner voice. Gandhi said that "... when it is the inner voice that speaks, it is unmistakable..."[107] I have learned this to be true, but it takes practice to be confident that you have distinguished your bias from what your inner voice is telling you.

Analyze and compare the facts, principles, and the revelations of God and make sure that they are all consistent with each other. Then identify what you think is the truth.

In the final analysis, one must make a decision, after honestly considering the facts and sound principles, according to his inner voice and spiritual awareness. This action transcends the physical senses. It is a spiritual experience.

Courageously choose to believe what you have found to be true, align your belief with the truth, and make any opinion adjustments as necessary.

Test your belief again against reliable standards for truth. Be open to new information or facts or insight. Sometimes you will have been wrong. But with persistence and practice you will get better and better at discerning truth, until it will become second nature to you.

Take action. Step forward with faith and align your behavior with your newfound knowledge.

Share and defend your knowledge of the truth.

A clear mind

In the end, truth is spiritually discerned. This discernment transcends the senses. For this process to occur, the mind must be unencumbered from personal consideration and bias. It must be free from external corrupting influence. The use of mind-altering substances of any kind, or addictive behavior, or the vices of the flesh, corrupt the mind and spirit 's facility to discern the pure light of truth. A rebellious attitude or a prideful heart likewise obstruct the mind from discerning truth. In a world distracted with artificial and counterfeit emotion created by substance abuse and carnal, petty and shallow entertainment, reality becomes ever more tainted and disguised. The current craze for "virtual reality," displayed in social media and video games, etc., can be an insidious and dangerous impediment to the mind's perception of what is real.

Strategies for *Testing* Truth

The sincere seeker of truth will test his beliefs against reliable standards of truth. As he considers his own human fallibility, he will recognize that he must frequently, if not continually, test his beliefs, be open to new information, and be ready and willing to change his beliefs to conform to truth. This is the path of honesty and integrity. This is not the same as doubting the revelation of truth to your heart. It is simply testing and reinforcing the conviction of truth that you possess. The honest seeker of truth will eagerly and willingly engage in this process.

Here are some suggestions for testing the truth of a particular proposition or belief:

- Do the reasons for my belief rest on any false standards for truth? (See Chapter 6, "False Standards and Impediments to Truth).

- Have I consulted trusted sources, and have I considered their counsel?

- Are my biases and/or emotions and self-interests affecting my belief?

- Does my belief conform to known facts?

- Is my belief consistent with time-honored and reliable moral values, such as honesty, respect for others, and love for others?

- Is my belief consistent with time-honored and reliable basic principles, such as free agency, and accountability?

- Is my belief consistent with the revelations of God?

- Am I listening to the "still small voice" within my heart?

- Am I able to distinguish my still small voice, or spiritual awareness, from my bias and/or emotions?

- Am I willing to give up my beliefs that are not true, even the ones I cherish?

- Am I willing to give up any behaviors or actions that are not consistent with the truth?

- Do I love the truth?

- Do I have the confirmation of my conscience that my belief is true?

- Does my belief sustain repeated scrutiny and continual testing?

- Am I willing to share and defend the knowledge that I have?

Here is an example from my own personal experience of when a "revelation" needs to be tested:

I was intent on ratifying my desire to cultivate a romantic relationship outside of my marriage. (See chapter "A Season of Adversity and Testing") I had met a person with whom I thought I was in love and had made plans to pursue that relationship. My thinking was that I had fallen out of love with my wife and deserved to find true love. I intensely wanted to do this, and I felt all of the rapture, anticipation, excitement and promise of a new romance.

I really thought I had a revelation when I felt a wave of deep emotion that seemed to confirm that I was doing the right thing. It came while I was at work, and all my thoughts were of my new infatuation. I was intently searching for validation. It came as a wave of excitement, almost a tingling all over. It was very powerful, and I still remember how intense the feeling was.

I acted on it because it was consistent with what I wanted to do. Well, it didn't turn out so well. It turned out to be a disaster for me, my family and my children, my church membership, and turned my life into a mess. This was either a message from an unknown source or trickery that my mind played upon me. This was a false revelation.

In retrospect, I could have tested it against the standards set out above and in this book:

The fact of the situation was that my proposed behavior didn't conform to revealed standards of behavior, "Thou shalt not commit adultery." But, it didn't necessarily conflict with the moral standards of our present culture, and I used this to rationalize that I was a special case.

My actions were contrary to all the values and principles that I had endorsed in the past. Values such as loyalty, honesty, obedience to God's commandments. And, it violated a fundamental principle to be faithful to one's marriage vows.

The "revelation" that I thought I had received was a strong *emotion* associated with the excitement of a new romance, that I confused with spiritual inspiration. It was what I *wanted* to believe. That is different from the pure, uplifting, enlightenment that leads one to do what is right. Looking back, I can distinguish that now. In short, I was deceived. I was a fool, pure and simple.

So, on all three counts, it was a false revelation.

It was a costly and disastrous mistake, but one that could have been prevented by a willingness to do what is right, to believe what is true, and to measure the issue against proven standards of truth, all of which directed the opposite course

18

Learning by Faith

"For faith is the substance of things hoped for, the evidence of things not
seen."[108] -- Hebrews 11:1

With Science, we learn by observing facts with our physical senses, proposing hypotheses that fit the facts, then testing the hypotheses in the physical world. When the evidence verifies the hypothesis, we conclude the proposition proven to be true. It's a very tangible and clear-cut process.

However, there are other times when observation of the facts is less defined. The appearance of the facts may be less tangible, more relative, often incomplete, and the truth sometimes more difficult to discover. Then, we must rely also on values, principles, our inner voice, and the revelations of God.

This requires faith.

"There are subjects where reason cannot take us far and we have to accept things on faith. Faith, then, does not contradict reason but transcends it"[109] --Gandhi

Thus, in our search for the truth of things, we may not always see clearly at first--then we must reach through the fog of uncertainty, relying on the facts that we do know, the values and principles that we have confidence in, while listening carefully to our inner voice, in a forward action of hope and faith, until we see clearly the light of truth. This is what is meant by the phrase, "learning by faith," and is crucial to the learning process.

"Faith is not to have a perfect knowledge of things; therefore if ye have faith ye hope for things which are not seen, which are true." [110] Alma 32:21

It requires that we have a hope in the Author of all truth, and that we are willing to believe in God. We then enlist His influence and guidance in our journey, as a headlamp in the darkness, and our minds become illuminated as we step forward onto the path of truth.

"Belief is the foundation of truth, we cannot possess something that we do not believe in. Belief takes a leap of faith. Given this necessity for leaping we are bound to sometimes leap in the wrong direction. I believe that this is the cause of much of our people's delusion. We have been blessed with free agency and therefore must bear the responsibility for leaping into darkness. Many find great despair in this, but I think that it is a beautiful thing, for the powers that be, God, must see some bravery in the fact that we leap at all." --David Gatten[111]

As we press forward, seeking truth, learning from our mistakes, testing, recalibrating, and persisting, we inexorably learn by faith the reality and truth of things.

Those who require tangible proof and substantiation in every step, and in every action on the path of learning, will never arrive with confidence to a sure knowledge of what is true. "Faith never demands an answer to every question but seeks assurance and courage to move forward, sometimes acknowledging, 'I don't know everything, but I do know enough to continue on the path of discipleship.'"[112]

This does not mean that we blindly grope forward with a vain hope that we are on the right path. This is not blind obedience and action, but "enlightened" obedience and action. It is based first upon our willingness to believe in God, to look to Him, and place our confidence in the first steps and elements that we know to be true. We then build on that with an open heart and mind, willing to honor with action the revelation of truth to our souls. After the test of our faith, by believing what is true, our belief matures into knowledge: corroboration, verification, and substantiation come as a flood of understanding, and we revel in the divine process and in the exhilaration of confidence that we know what is true. This process extends our imagination, teaches us to act, expands our knowledge, and prepares us to do good in ever greater circles of influence.

"...if thou canst believe, all things are possible to him that believeth."[113] --
Mark 9:23

19

Defend the Truth

Once you have discovered truth and made a commitment to believe it, you have a sacred obligation to live it, share it and defend it. Why would you want to hold the truth close only for yourself, and not live it and share it with others?

"How can you believe in a moral or religious precept and not live it?

"The gulf between word and belief is untruth. The dissonance between creed and deed is the root of innumerable wrongs in our civilization; it is the weakness of all churches, states, parties, and persons. It gives institutions and men split personalities."[114] --Louis Fischer, *The Life of Mahatma Ghandi*

As a precious possession, bought at a great price, surely it becomes our duty to share. Our mission thus enlarges and expands from finding and believing, to knowing, to living, to sharing, and thence to defending the truth.

Sharing and defending the truth requires humility and courage. As you stand for the truth, you become a light to the world that will not be unnoticed. You stand for truth, not by flashy, flamboyant statements, but by the small acts of integrity in your everyday life that are consistent with the values and principles and knowledge that you enjoy, and when called upon, humbly and carefully assert what you know to be true. The attention to you for standing for truth may bring increased scrutiny that requires careful awareness of your example. You must be consistent in your behavior to avoid accusation of inconsistency or hypocrisy. More than ever before, you will be judged by your actions, not only by your words. You must avoid even the appearance of evil and live to be above reproach.

Thus, the challenge to share and defend truth places an even greater burden upon the seeker of truth to honor the priceless gift by righteous living.

What can you expect in return for sharing and defending truth?

A clear conscience, a joyful heart, and the approbation of your Maker. Certainly, you cannot expect to be applauded by the world at large, which is falling headlong into selfishness and the petty wisdom of men. Indeed, your doctrine may be at odds with the conventional wisdom and behavior and will testify sharply as to the foolishness and futility of the powers that promote the shallow and false philosophies of the times.

It may invite argument, ridicule, and even persecution. You will be misconstrued and misunderstood. But you need not fear. "To be great is to be misunderstood,"[115] said Ralph Waldo Emerson.

Truth is on your side, and you will be confident amidst the storms and adversities of opposition. You will stand tall, independent, strong, and sure, as the stature of your manhood rises above and in contrast to, the weak and insincere proponents of deception and falsehood.

The Power of Truth

"A man cannot truly believe in God without believing in the final inevitable triumph of Truth. If you have Truth on your side you can pass through the dark valley of slander misrepresentation and abuse, undaunted, as though you wore a magic suit of mail that no bullet could enter, no arrow could pierce. You can hold your head high, toss it fearlessly and defiantly, look every man calmly and unflinchingly in the eye, as though you rode, a victorious king, returning at the head of your legions with banners waving and lances glistening, and bugles filling the air with music. You can feel the great expansive wave of moral health surging through you as the quickened blood courses through the body of him who is gladly, gloriously proud of physical health. You will know that all will come right in the end, that it must come, that error must flee before the great white light of truth, as darkness slinks away into nothingness in the presence of the sunburst. Then, with Truth as your guide, your companion, your ally, and inspiration, you tingle with the consciousness of your kinship with the Infinite and all the petty trials, sorrows and sufferings of life fade away like temporary, harmless visions seen in a dream."[116]

--William George Jordan, The Power of Truth

The good and great will be attracted to your side, and surely join you in the great cause in which you are engaged. You will find the greatest thrill, and the most exquisite satisfaction, knowing you are on the side of truth. Your understanding and wisdom will amplify with your experience, and you will find the most precious desires of your heart blossom to fruition in the majestic advance of righteousness and truth.

In the grand battle of defense of the truth, keep these principles in mind:

Love your neighbor. Your defense of truth will have no power to change the world without the love of mankind. Indeed, the very nature of truth only operates in the sphere of love and kindness for other people. This will manifest our true commitment to truth as we bear with patience the perceived weaknesses and foibles of others. We all have our blind spots, and the true friend of mankind will make tender and sympathetic allowances for others, hoping that they will also make the same allowances for him. "Truth should ever extend the hand of love; never the hand clenching a bludgeon."[117] -- William George Jordan

Eschew hatred and violence. Demonization of our opponents is always counterproductive, and ineffective. It offends the very essence of truth. It damages our own credibility. When we demonize our opponents, they will find it almost impossible to listen to us, and certainly not the motivation to follow us. This is different than disagreeing with our opponents or pointing out false or hypocritical positions. It simply means that we always treat others with respect, with civil discourse, and do not descend to the ugliness of name-calling and hatred, or worse, to the futility and destruction of violence. Unlawful violence is never the answer.

We must rely on **rational dialogue** to convince each other of wise policy, rather than forcing our will upon others. When one party tries to game (manipulate) the system to achieve power and force their agenda, the other party is aggrieved, resentful, and this leads to polarization and even, perhaps, to violence. A recent political candidate stated, "we cannot change people's minds—we must change the system." This is exactly backward. If we are to effect lasting change, we must change peoples' hearts and minds. "A man convinced against his will is of the same opinion still."[118]

We must not tolerate evil, but we can be tolerant of others' human weakness, for we surely have our own deficiencies. As we are gentle and tolerant of the human differences of others, we create space for patience, mutual appreciation and understanding, and that will enable us to approach unity in belief, purpose, and action. "The tenderness of tolerance will illuminate and glorify the world, --as moonlight makes all things beautiful, --if we will only permit it."[119]—Jordan

Lies, falsehoods and deceit must be challenged and defeated. It takes courage to identify and call out hypocrisy, deception, wrong behavior, and falsity, but the power of truth is such that in doing so with a clear voice, without guile, the truth transcends the petty arguments of deceptive interests, and sheds light and understanding to the honest of heart.

Avenues for defending the truth:

- Teach your children correct principles, based on the values and principles that you have chosen to guide your life.[120]
- Share your perspective and knowledge with family and friends.
- Be an example of a truth-seeker in social and work settings by your example of careful rectitude, open-mindedness, tolerance of other person's opinions, kindness and patience.
- Use social media to appropriately express what you have found to be true.
- Take a public stand on important issues of the day in defense of the truth.
- Find your particular niche and discover your own unique talent and calling to enlighten the world, whether it be a poet, a musician, a writer, a mother or father, or a good worker.
- "Do what you do, do well."[121] Teach the world what excellence looks like as you honor the truth in all you do.
- Be a witness of God and Jesus Christ.
- Keep His commandments and live a life of virtue.

The Cost—the Sacrifice

One must not expect that the path of truth is an easy one, free from obstacles, opposition, difficulty, or even persecution. It has always been so. The cause of truth has always extracted a price, perhaps even in proportion to its relevance and importance. We must be prepared to pay that price.

What is the cost that one must pay to find and defend the truth?

What is the sacrifice that one must place on the altar of Life to obtain knowledge of things as they really are?

Martyrs of all ages have sacrificed their very lives in defense of truth. Others have sacrificed their fortunes, their good name, their friends and even families--all that they possessed, in this grand purpose.

For us, the sacrifice may be only of our time, our commitment, and our effort to become informed and seek out the truth. Perhaps the sacrifice will be of our own bias, our own selfish interests, and our own intense want to believe according to our own, selfish and personal agenda.

20

You May Know the Truth of All Things

"And when ye shall receive these things, I would exhort you that ye would ask God, the Eternal Father, in the name of Christ, if these things are not true, and if ye shall ask with a sincere heart, with real intent, having faith in Christ, he will manifest the truth of it unto you, by the power of the Holy Ghost. And by the power of the Holy Ghost ye may know the truth of all things."[122]

-- Book of Mormon, Moroni 10:4-5

I have always been intrigued by this scripture. Yes, it's possible to know the truth of one thing. But here is the key to knowing what is true about all things. That is the promise of God to those who follow this path. And the path is what we have been describing—searching, seeking, and asking for light.

As we seek to know the truth with real intent, we will be led on the sure path toward knowledge. This is every man's test, and the supreme challenge for his life.

The path of truth is a straight and narrow path. It is a rigorous discipline that requires commitment to a higher, exacting, and unyielding standard. That is the way it has to be. There is plenty of room for mistakes, diversions, and the weaknesses that we are all subject to, but with consistent and persistent effort, repentance, recalibration, and patience, the genuine seeker will find his way.

As truth unfolds in one's mind, it becomes delicious and precious. The experience expands his mind and opens his heart and enlarges his soul. He learns and comprehends the peaceable things. This is one of life's sweetest and most sublime experiences and lifts one above the monotony and drudgery of his everyday routine to exciting new vistas of knowledge and purpose, one that exalts his imagination, his vision, and his view of things as they really are, and as they will be.

The Challenge

The challenge to each of us is this: Open your soul to the truth. Strive to find the truth. Seek the truth with all of your energy, commitment, and strength. Choose to believe it. Be willing to sacrifice all, but actually begin making the sacrifice now, by giving up your pride, your selfishness, your self-interest, your biases--whatever is necessary-- in the grand search and glorious defense of truth. Then, with a broken heart, a contrite spirit, in the spirit of obedience and real intent, with faith in the Author of truth, press forward with joy and confidence, a day-by-day journey that will end in the Perfect Day. Then, you will surely have learned in full measure that "The Truth will make you free."

The Power to do Good

As you take on the challenge of passionately seeking truth, you will glimpse the realities of eternity, and begin to have access to the Power that moves the universe. As you follow this path, you will find yourself invigorated and inspired above your natural abilities, and, sensing the power of truth that infuses all righteous action, you will join the divine forces of the universe in accomplishing good, and in creating ever-expanding panoramas of Life, joy and happiness.

This quest is a sacred and holy pursuit that transcends the selfish interests and mundane moments of our own lives and leads us step-by-step to our ultimate destiny. This is the destiny of man.

"For behold, this is my work and my glory, to bring to pass the immortality and eternal life of man."[123]

21

The Victory of Truth

The Truth will prevail.

In the great war between truth and error, perpetuated since the beginning of time, the truth will claim the ultimate victory, because that is the very nature of things. This is the reality of the Eternal Law: the elemental nature of substances, actions, intentions, and events. This is the Law of the universe.

What is it about Truth that eventually wins the battle? What is it about truth that conquers deception, error, and the accumulated energy and power of falsehood?

Truth is light. The light of truth, like the sun shining from behind the clouds, eventually breaks forth, and cannot long be hidden. As the day follows night, as the brilliance of the sun shines and dissipates the shadow of the storm, so does the illumination of truth defeat the darkness, gloom, and confusion of deceit and evil. It will ever be so.

The evolutions and seasons of nature teach the same—the renewal, exuberance and freshness of spring follows the barrenness and shadow of winter. All Nature in the revolving permanence of the cycles of life combines to teach the triumph of light, of reality, of accountability, of the conquest of Eternal Law. This we have learned that we may depend on.

Do not try to fool the universe. As we take the side of dishonesty, or falsity and error, we embark on a fruitless, futile, and impossible task that will leave us in failure and emptiness, our hopes blasted, alone, bereft, confused, and a slave to darkness and vice. We can never really harm the universe; we can only harm ourselves. "The only tragedy in this world my friend is sin" – and sin may be overcome through the infinite Atonement of Jesus Christ. No matter our most intense efforts to deceive or betray ourselves, despite the facade of shallow and evanescent success, the truth will come out. The light of reality will emerge and claim its own.

> "A little consideration of what takes place around us every day would show us that a higher law than that of our will regulates events; that our painful labors are unnecessary and fruitless; that only in our easy, simple, spontaneous action are we strong, and by contenting ourselves with obedience we become divine. Belief and love—a believing love will relieve us of a vast load of care. O my brothers, God exists. There is a soul at the centre of nature and over the will of every man, so that none of us can wrong the universe. It has so infused its strong enchantment into nature that we prosper when we accept its advice, and when we struggle to wound its creatures our hands are glued to our sides, or they beat our own breasts. The whole course of things goes to teach us faith. We need only obey. There is guidance for each of us, and by lowly listening we shall hear the right word."[124]
>
> -- Ralph Waldo Emerson

Do not be worried about the ultimate victory of right. "... let your hearts be comforted... for all flesh is in mine hands; be still and know that I am God." [125]

The history of nations, rulers, and of individuals bears out that the truth eventually prevails. Sooner or later, the lies, false philosophies, corrupted traditions, and evil doings come to light. Nations are known for what they were. The pride and arrogance of the Greeks proved their ruination. The corruption and decadence of Rome eventually destroyed that great civilization. The evil of Adolph Hitler resurged in his last hours of despair, futility, and ruin. The murderous rule of Stalin is well documented in The Gulag Archipelago and ended with his insanity and lonely, agonizing death. Rulers are known by history for their evil (and righteous) doings. Plutarch aptly recorded the lives of many Greeks and Romans. Their virtues and vices stand exposed for all time.

Individuals are known for who they really are as the passage of time and events illuminate their actions and character. Every right and good act will be rewarded, and man will be held accountable for every wrong and evil act. "Though the mills of God grind slowly, yet they grind exceeding small; Though with patience He stands waiting, with exactness grinds He all."[126]

I have personally experienced the victory of truth manifest in a great contest of reality and truth, vs blame and offense, when I was sued in court for the unfortunate death of one of my patients. Many circumstantial particulars made me look liable, and the plaintiff took full advantage to paint a picture of negligence and incompetence. But in the full exposition of events and details, in a context of honesty, integrity, and sincere intentions, what really happened came to light. This overpowered the negative and accusatory narrative of self-interest and hatred. The event resolved in the enlightenment of the jury to a verdict of innocence. This was only possible in a setting of transparency, honesty and integrity. I had determined at the outset that I would tell the truth, no matter how painful. There were several moments in the trial when the truth about extraneous events was less than favorable to me. I had to admit that I had made some unrelated mistakes of judgment, and, as I consulted with my attorney and prepared to make full disclosure of an embarrassing event, the plaintiff's attorney suddenly and inexplicably became confused and the issue passed without further notice. But, knowing that I was fully prepared for full and honest disclosure gave me confidence in my own integrity. After the trial, my attorneys told me unequivocally that it was essentially my character that convinced the jury to a verdict of innocence.

Truth overcomes circumstances. In such a setting, the power of truth is powerfully manifested--a perception of the "still, small voice" that divides light from darkness and simply overpowers error.

So, what of the skeptic, of the liar, the purveyor of false and evil philosophies, or of the tyrant, or the villain? What of the short-sighted and self-deceptive efforts of humanity to short-circuit the truth? What of the little lies that we each flatter ourselves with to rationalize our personal violations of what is right? How is it that humanity persists in fooling itself into its own petty declarations, private opinions, and formulations of what is true—against all history, experience, and divine revelation to the contrary?

This is the enduring question of human civilization. Why do we not learn? Why do we persist in the same lies, deceptions, and falsehoods of our fathers? Why do we betray our very identity as we embrace our own selfish, yet clearly debunked and discredited notions that direct our lives?

We must learn for ourselves. In this grand experiment of life for each individual, he must learn what is real, and exercise his faith to find and embrace the truth. As he uses his God-given agency to choose, he must find his way and prove his own integrity and commitment to truth. As he does this, he learns for himself the laws of the universe, rises to his full stature as a son or daughter of God, and prepares himself for his ultimate destiny. The greatest victory of Truth is when each individual learns to discern for himself the truth, and chooses of his own volition to walk that "straight and narrow path" of faith in Jesus Christ that inexorably leads to the knowledge of all things as they really are, to the peaceable things, to the glorious expansion of intellect, self-awareness and understanding. This transports him in a flood of brilliant light and of infinite love to the presence of the Source of all truth, God, the Eternal Father, as an heir to all that the Father hath: thrones, kingdoms, principalities, powers, creations, and eternal life. May it be so for each of us.

Appendix 1

Blind Men and the Elephant

by John Godfrey Saxe (1816–1887)

It was six men of Indostan

To learning much inclined,

Who went to see the Elephant

(Though all of them were blind),

That each by observation

Might satisfy his mind.

The First approached the Elephant,

And happening to fall

Against his broad and sturdy side,

At once began to bawl:

God bless me! but the Elephant

Is very like a wall!

The Second, feeling of the tusk,

Cried, Ho! what have we here

So very round and smooth and sharp?

To me tis mighty clear

This wonder of an Elephant

Is very like a spear!

Appendix

The Third approached the animal,
And happening to take
The squirming trunk within his hands,
Thus boldly up and spake:
I see, quoth he, the Elephant
Is very like a snake!

The Fourth reached out an eager hand,
And felt about the knee.
What most this wondrous beast is like
Is mighty plain, quoth he;
'Tis clear enough the Elephant
Is very like a tree!

The Fifth, who chanced to touch the ear,
Said: Even the blindest man
Can tell what this resembles most;
Deny the fact who can
This marvel of an Elephant
Is very like a fan!?

The Sixth no sooner had begun
About the beast to grope,
Than, seizing on the swinging tail
That fell within his scope,
I see, quoth he, the Elephant

Is very like a rope!

And so these men of Indostan
Disputed loud and long,
Each in his own opinion
Exceeding stiff and strong,
Though each was partly in the right,
And all were in the wrong!

Moral:

So oft in theologic wars,
The disputants, I ween,
Rail on in utter ignorance
Of what each other mean,
And prate about an Elephant
Not one of them has seen!

158

Appendix 2

Recommended further perusal (my favorite selections):

Video

" Epic Talk - What is Truth?" by Dieter F. Uchtdorf , Jan 19, 2013 #truth#epictalk

Jordan Peterson, Harvard talk, 4/10//2017: "Post modernism and the Mask of Compassion"

Books

The Plays of Sophocles

War and Peace by Leo Tolstoy

Les Miserables by Victor Hugo

A Tale of Two Cities by Charles Dickens

The Prairie Years and the War Years, by Carl Sandburg

The Decline and Fall of the Roman Empire, by Edward Gibbon

The Rise and Fall of the Third Reich, by William L. Shirer

Fathers and Sons, by Ivan Turgenev

The Trial and Death of Socrates, Plato

The Gulag Archipelago by Aleksander I. Solzhenitsyn

The Life and Times of Jesus Christ, by Alfred Edersheim

The Life of Christ, by Frederic W. Farrar, D.D., F.R.S.

Democracy and America, by Alexis de Tocqueville

Heroes and Hero Worship, by Thomas Carlyle

Scott's Last Expedition by Captain R.R. Scott

The Life of Mahatma Gandhi, by Louis Fischer

Spiritual Roots of Human Relations, by Stephen R. Covey

Jesus the Christ, by James E. Talmage

The Power of Truth, by William George Jordan

Crime and Punishment, by Dostoevsky

The Idiot, by Dostoevsky

Anna Karenina by Leo Tolstoy

How to Win Friends and Influence People, by Dale Carnegie

The Power of Positive Thinking, by Norman Vincent Peale

The Way to God, Selected Writing from Mahatma Gandhi

Nature, by Ralph Waldo Emerson

As a Man Thinketh, by James Allen

The Writings of C.S. Lewis

Still the Best Hope, by Dennis Prager

Representative Men, by Ralph Waldo Emerson

The History of the Life of M. Tullius Cicero, by Conyers Middleton, D.D.

The Book Thief, by Markus Zusak

The Holy Bible, King James Version

The Book of Mormon

Ivanhoe, by Sir Walter Scott

Walden, by Hendry David Thoreau

The Talisman, by Sir Walter Scott

Plutarch's Lives, by Plutarch

Out of My Life and Thought, by Albert Schweitzer

Black Night, White Snow, by Harrison E. Salisbury

The Golden Bough, by Sir James George Frazer

Alone, by Richard E. Byrd

Wilderness Essays by John Muir

Macbeth, by William Shakespeare

Othello, by William Shakespeare

Moby Dick by Herman Melville

Essays, by Ralph Waldo Emerson

The Wonders of the Arctic World, A history of all the researches and discoveries in the

Appendix

Frozen Regions of the North, by Epes Sargent, Esq.

Poems

I Wandered, Lonely as a Cloud, by William Wordsworth

To a Waterfowl, by William Cullen Bryant

The Rhodora, by Ralph Waldo Emerson

The Ballad of Reading Gaol, by Oscar Wilde

Mending Wall, By Robert Frost

The Road Not Taken, by Robert Frost

The Snowstorm, by Ralph Waldo Emerson

Death, be not Proud, by John Donne

Days, by Ralph Waldo Emerson

Grass, by Carl Sandburg

Recessional, by Rudyard Kipling

Frost at Midnight, by Samuel Taylor Coleridge

Music

Canon in D by Johann Pachelbel

18th Variation from Rhapsody On a Theme of Paganini, Op. 43, by Rachmaninoff

Morning Has Broken, words by Eleanor Farjeon, performed by Cat Stevens, 1971

America the Beautiful, by Katharine Lee Bates

Battle Hymn of the Republic by Julia Ward Howe

Blue Danube by Johann Straus

Hallelujah Chorus by George Frederick Handel

How Great Thou Art, words by Carl Boberg

The Holy City, Victorian ballad, music by Michael Maybrick

Que Sera Sera, by Jay Livingston and Ray Evans, performed by Doris Day, 1956

Amazing Grace, words by John Newton

Back Home Again by John Denver

The Peace Carol by John Denver

The Swan, by Camille Saint-Saens

Both Sides Now, by Judy Collins

Seasons in the Sun, by The Kingston Trio

Lay Me Down, by Loretta Lynn and Willie Nelson

O Holy Night, composed by Adolphe Adam, words by Placide Cappeau

Silent Night, words by Franz Xaver Gruber, lyrics by Joseph Mohr

The Impossible Dream by Mitch Leigh

I Know that My Redeemer Lives, words by Samuel Medley, Music by Lewis D. Edwards

Blowin' In the Wind, by Peter, Paul, and Mary

Panis Angelicus by Cesar Franck

Against the Wind, by Bob Seger, performed by Willie Nelson

Do What You Do Do Well, by Ned Miller

162

Appendix 3

A personal declaration—a personal testimony:

I do not know the truth of all things, and I have much to learn. But I do have knowledge of these few things, knowledge that I have learned of myself to be true.

I know that as one opens his soul to the truth, it's possible to discern truth in this chaotic and confusing world. I have experienced this many times.

I know that's it's possible to banish false standards of truth and to distinguish my bias and emotion from the "still small voice" of the revelation of God to my soul.

I know that God lives, and that He is my Heavenly Father. I know that He loves me, and I love Him.

I know that Jesus is the Christ, the Son of God, and my Redeemer. I have experienced the miracle of His Redeeming Power in my life.

I know that the Holy Ghost teaches and testifies of truth. He has witnessed to me the truth of many things, not only of purely religious matters, but those of my everyday life. I know that the revelation of the Spirit of God, or the Holy Ghost, to my soul is real, and I can trust that revelation.

I know that God speaks to his prophets who have recorded his words to the human family in the Holy Scriptures, and that He continues to reveal his will to prophets in our own time. I know that they are true prophets.

I know that God is the Creator of this world, and that all Nature testifies of Him and is symbolic of Him and his great and marvelous works.

I know that God hears and answers my prayers.

I know that following the commandments of God brings joy and happiness, and that as I follow the path of righteousness and faith, I am able to find and believe the truth.

I believe that as I seek with real intent, having faith in Jesus Christ, and obeying His commandments, I may know the truth of all things.[127]

I love the truth. I am willing to give up all that I have and am so that I might have knowledge of what is true.

These statements are consistent with all the evidences and facts that I have observed in my lifetime, and the values and principles which I have learned to be sound and dependable. Above all, I know them by the revelation of God to my soul. I have tested them, and they have always held true.

BIBLIOGRAPHY

Adams, James T., et al, *Living Philosophies;* New York: Simon and Shuster, 1931

Bowen, *Miracle at Philadelphia, the Story of the Constitutional Convention May to September 1787;* New York: Book-of-the-Month Club, Little, Brown and Company, 1986

Bronowski, Jacob, *The Ascent of Man;* London: The Folio Society, MMXII

Byrd, Richard E., Admiral, *Alone;* Covelo, California: Island Press, 1984

Carlyle, Thomas, *On Heroes, Hero-Worship, and the Heroic in History;* Chicago: A.C. McClurg and Company, 1905

Book of Mormon, The; Salt Lake City: The Church of Jesus Christ of Latter-Day Saints, 1986

Carnegie, Dale, *How to Win Friends and Influence People*, New York: Simon & Schuster 1964

Copan, Paul, *True for You, But Not for Me: Overcoming Objections to Christian Faith;* Minneapolis, Minnesota: Bethany House Publishers, 2009

Doctrine and Covenants of The Church of Jesus Christ of Latter-Day Saints, The; Salt Lake City: The Church of Jesus Christ of Latter-Day Saints, 2013

Durant, Will, *The Life of Greece, The Story of Civilization: 2;* Norwalk, Connecticut: The Easton Press, 1939, 1966

Emerson, Ralph Waldo, *The Essays of Ralph Waldo Emerson*, (The Illustrated Modern Library); Random House, Inc., 1944

Emerson, Ralph Waldo, *The Works of Ralph Waldo Emerson;* London: MacMillan and Co., 1897

Emerson, Ralph Waldo, *Nature;* Aurora, New York: Roycroft Shop, 1905

Fischer, Louis, *The Life of Mahatma Gandhi*, Norwalk, Conn.: The Easton Press, 1988

Gandhi, Mahatma, *The Way to God, Selected Writings from Mahatma Gandhi*, Berkeley, California: Atlantic Books, 2009

BIBLIOGRAPHY

Goethe, Johann Wolfgang, von, *Goethe's Autobiography, Poetry and Truth from My Own Life*; Washington, D.C.: Public Affairs Press, 1949

Hayek, F.A., *The Road to Serfdom* (The Classics of Liberty Library); Chicago: Gryphon Corp., 2016

Holy Bible, The, King James Edition

Jordan, William George, *The Power of Truth*; The Deseret Book Company, 1952

Kirk, Russell, *The Conservative Mind*; Chicago: Regnery Books, 1986

Levin, Mark R., *Unfreedom of the Press*, New York: Threshold Editions, 2019

Lewis, C.S., *The Problem of Pain*, New York: The MacMillan Co., 1967

Maus, Cynthia Pearl, *Christ and the Fine Arts*, New York: Harper & Brothers, 1938

Mill, John Stuart, *On Liberty*; Norwalk, Conn.: The Easton Press, 1991

Nibley, Hugh, *The Ancient State*; Salt Lake City: Deseret Book Co., 1991

Nibley, Hugh, *Enoch the Prophet*; Salt Lake City: Deseret Book Co., 1986

Nibley, Hugh, *The World and the Prophets*; Salt Lake City: Deseret Book Co., 1987

Pearl of Great Price, The; The Church of Jesus Christ of Latter-Day Saints

Plato, *The Apology*

Plato, *Lysis, or Friendship, The Symposium, Phaedrus*; Norwalk, Conn.: The Easton Press, 1979

Plato, *The Republic*; Franklin Center, PA: The Franklin Library, 1975

Plato, *Plato IX, Timaeus, Critias, Cleitophon, Menexenus, Epistles*; Loeb Classical Library, MCMLXXV

Plutarch, *Plutarch's Morals*; New York: The Athenaeum Society

Sahakian, William S., and Sahakian, Mabel Lewis, *Ideas of the Great Philosophers*; Barnes & Noble, 1968

Scott, Richard,

Shapiro, Ben, *The Right Side of History—How Reason and Moral Purpose Made the West Great*; Broadside Books, 2019

Simon, Roger L., *I Know Best, How Moral Narcissism is Destroying Our Republic, if It*

BIBLIOGRAPHY

Hasn't Already; New York: Encounter Books, 2016

Solzhenitsyn, Aleksandr I., *The Gulag Archipelago 1918-1956, An Experiment in Literary Investigation I-II*; New York: Harper & Rowe, 1973

Sophocles, *The Plays of Sophocles*; The Franklin Library, 1980

Wilson, James Q., *The Moral Sense*, The Free Press, 1993

Notes

1 *The New Testament,* (King James Version), Philippians 4:7

2 *The New Testament,* (King James Version), I Corinthians 2:7

3 Neal A. Maxwell, "The Tugs and Pulls of the World," General Conference Address, The Church of Jesus Christ of Latter-Day Saints, Nov. 2000.

4 See Paul Copan, *True for You, But Not for Me: Overcoming Objections to Christian Faith,* Minneapolis, Minn: Bethany House Publishers; 2009, for an excellent discussion of this point.

5 William S. Sahakian and Mabel Lewis Sahakian, *Ideas of the Great Philosophers,* Barnes & Noble, 1968, p 28

6 *The Doctrine & Covenants of The Church of Jesus Christ of Latter-Day Saints*, Salt Lake City, Utah, 2013 by Intellectual Reserve, Inc., Section 93:24

7 *The New Testament,* (King James version), Hebrews 4:12

8 Mahatma Gandhi, *The Way to God, Selected Writings from Mahatma Gandhi;* North Atlantic Books, Berkeley, California, 2009, p 67

9 from Sophocles, "Antigone", *The Plays of Sophocles*; The Franklin Library, Franklin Center, Pennsylvania, 1980, p 193

10 Earl of Rochester, "A Satire Against Mankind", quoted in *Goethe's Autobiography,* p 512

11 *The New Testament,* 1 Corinthians 13:12

12 John Godfrey Saxe, "Blind Men and the Elephant"

13 Francis Bacon, *Novum Organum*

14 Roger L. Simon, *I Know Best, How Moral Narcissism is Destroying Our Republic, If It Hasn't Already,* Encounter Books, New York, 2016, p 11

15 *Doctrine & Covenants,* Section 93:39

16 Justice Anthony Kennedy, 2016

17 Carlyle, Thomas, *On Heroes, Hero-Worship, and the Heroic in History,* A.C. McClurg and Company, Chicago, 1905, p 10

18 Ibid., p 12

19 *Doctrine & Covenants,* Section 93:31

20 Ralph Waldo Emerson, *The Essays of Ralph Waldo Emerson,* "Intellect", *The Illustrated Modern Library,* p 199

21 Dinesh D'Souza, lecture at Texas A&M University, Oct 17, 2018

22 John Stuart Mill, *On Liberty,* The Easton Press, 1991, p 31-32

23 Joe Biden, Speech at Iowa State Fair, August 8, 2019

24 Mark Levin, *Unfreedom of the Press,* (referencing Andrew Malcom's opinion piece, "Media's Anti-Trump Addiction Amps Up the Outrage and Fuels the Public's Suspicion," *The Miami Herald*, January 15, 2019) Threshold Editions, 2019, p 67,68

25 Russell Kirk, *The Conservative Mind* (Chicago, Regnery Books, 1986), p 29

26 *The New Testament,* Romans 12:3, 1 Corinthians 12:7; *The Book of Mormon,* 2 Nephi 2:5

27 Johann Wolfgang von Goethe, *Goethe's Autobiography, Poetry and Truth From My Own Life,* Public Affairs Press, 1949, p 603

28 *The Doctrine & Covenants,* Section 8:2

29 Aleksandr I. Solzhenitsyn, *The Gulag Archipelago 1918-1956, An Experiment in Literary Investigation I-II,* translated from the Russian by Thomas P. Whitney; Harper & Row, 1973, pp 185-186

30 *The Book of Mormon,* 2 Nephi 2:5, The Church of Jesus Christ of Latter-Day Saints,

31 Nibley, Hugh, *The Ancient State,* "Three Shrines, Mantic, Sophic, and Sophistic," Deseret Book Company, Salt Lake City, 1991, p 327

32 Ibid., p 371

33 Ibid., p 319

34 Plato, "The Apology," 33C

35 Plato, *The Republic,* Book VII, Franklin Center, PA: The Franklin Library, 1975

36 Nibley, *The Ancient State,* p 340

37 Gandhi, *The Way to God, Selected Writing from Mahatma Gandhi;* Berkeley, California: Atlantic Books, 2009, p 25

38 Gandhi, *The Way to God,* p 67

39 Solzhenitsyn, p 174

40 Jacob Bronowski, *The Ascent of Man,* The Folio Society, London, MMXII, pp 240-241

41 Jonah Goldberg, "Jonah Goldberg: Belief Now Outweighs Truth in the Kavanaugh Hearings," St. *Louis Post-Dispatch,* Sept 26, 2018

42 Bret Stephens, "Believability is the Road to National Ruin," *New York Times,* Sep 28, 2018

43 Bret Stephens, "This I Believe about Blasey v Kavanaugh," *New York Times,* Sep 25, 2018

44 *The Book of Mormon,* 2 Nephi 9:28-29

45 *The Book of Mormon,* Moroni 7:12-18

46 *The New Testament,* Matthew 7:16

47 Jordan Peterson, "Identity Politics and the Marxist Lie of White Privilege," Youtube.com

48 *The New Testament,* Hebrews 10:35

49 John Jaques, "Oh Say, What Is Truth?" *Hymns of the Church of Jesus Christ of Latter-Day Saints,* Deseret Book Company, Salt Lake City, Utah, 1985, p 272

50 See John Stuart Mill, *On Liberty,* for an excellent discussion on how freedom of expression and argument is essential to the discovery of truth.

51 Hugh Nibley, *The World and the Prophets,"* Deseret Book Company, Salt Lake City, Utah, 1987, p 1

52 Ibid, p 10-11

53 (See Nibley, Chapter 10, p 80)

54 Ibid, p 78-79)

55 Nibley, *The Ancient State,* p 358

56 Plato, *Plato IX, Timaeus, Critias, Cleitophon, Menexenus, Epistles,* Loeb Classical Library, Translated by R.G. Bury, Harvard University Press, London, MCMLXXV, "Timaeus", p 55

57 Ibid, p. 189

58 Ralph Waldo Emerson, "Spiritual Laws," p 79

59 Benjamin Franklin, from Catherine Drinker Bowen's *Miracle at Philadelphia, The Story of the Constitutional Convention May to September 1787,* Book-of-the-Month Club, Little, Brown and Company, New York, 1986, p125-126

60 (see lecture given by Kevin Portteus, Larence Fertig Professor of Politics , Hillsdale College, "Congress, How it Worked and Why it Doesn't, 2019)

61 Mahatma Gandhi, "The Way to God," pp 45-46

62 Neal L. Anderson, "Faith is not by Chance, but by Choice," General Conference of the Church of Jesus Christ of Latter-Day Saints, November, 2015

63 *The Book of Mormon,* 2 Nephi 9:28,29

64 Will Durant, *The Life of Greece, The Story of Civilization: 2*; The Easton Press, 1939, 1966, p 642

65 Ibid, p 657

66 Shapiro, *The Right Side of History—How Reason and Moral Purpose Made the West Great*; Broadside Books, 2019, p 184-186

67 Ralph Waldo Emerson, "Character, 1866," *Lectures and Biographical Sketches, Complete Works,* vol. 10

68 Ralph Waldo Emerson, "Illusions," *The Works of Ralph Waldo Emerson*, Macmillan and Col, Ltd., New York, 1896, Vol V, pp 263-264

69 Gandhi, *The Way to God,* pp 25, 26

70 C.S. Lewis, *The Problem of Pain,* The MacMillan Company, New York, 1967, p 89

71 James Q. Wilson, *The Moral Sense,* New York: The Free Press, 1993, p 163

72 Samuel Taylor Coleridge, "Frost at Midnight"

73 *Doctrine and Covenants,* Section 76:10

74 Admiral Richard E. Byrd, *Alone,* Island Press, Covelo, California, 1984, p 120, 160, 161

75 Admiral Richard E. Byrd, *Alone,* p 161

76 Admiral Richard E. Byrd, *Alone,* p 178, 179

77 David Gatten, *personal communication, 2018*

78 Plato, *Plato: Lysis, or Friendship, The Symposium, Phaedrus,* The Easton Press, Norwalk, Connecticut, , 1979, p. 103

79 Ralph Waldo Emerson, "Nature", The Roycroft Shop, East Aurora, New York, 1905, pp 22,27,29

80 Gandhi, *The Way to God,* p 43

81 Richard G. Scott, *Finding Peace, Happiness, and Joy* (Salt Lake City: Deseret Book, 2014), 38

82 Boyd K. Packer "Teach the Scriptures," Teaching Seminary: Preservice Readings (2004) 74-76

83 Richard Le Gallienne, quoted in *Christ and the Fine Arts,* by Cynthia Pearl Maus, Haper & Brothers Publishers, New York, 1938, p I

84 Celia Thaxter, "The Voice of God," quoted in *Christ and the Fine Arts, p 20*

85 Michael Grunwald, "How everything became the culture war," *The Week,* Nov 22, 2018

86 Ben Shapiro, *The Right Side of History,* Broadside Books, 2019, p 73

87 Mark R. Levin, *Unfreedom of the Press,* (referencing Bill Kovach and Tom Rosenstiel, *The Elements of Journalism),* Threshold Editions, 2019, p 17

88 Ralph Waldo Emerson, "Politics," pp 336-341

89 *The New Testament,* Romans 8:28

90 Plutarch, *Plutarch's Morals,* "How to Profit by Our Enemies," translated from the Greek by several hands. Corrected and Revised by William W. Goodwin, Ph. D.; New York, The Athenaeum Society, Vol 1, p 293

91 Plutarch, 283-291

92 "Beijing to Judge Every Resident Based on Behavior by End of 2020," *Bloomberg News,* November 21, 2018

93 F.A. Hayek, *The Road to Serfdom,* THE CLASSICS OF LIBERTY LIBRARY, Gryphon Corp., 2016, p 231-232

94 *The New Testament,* Matthew 7:12

95 President Russell M Nelson, President of the Church of Jesus Christ of Latter-Day Saints, at the 100th annual national convention of the National Association for the Advancement of Colored People (NAACP).

96 Jacob Bronowski, *The Ascent of Man,* The Folio Society, London, 2012, p 227

97 Ibid, p 230

98 Hugh Nibley, *Enoch the Prophet,* "The Book of Enoch as a Theodicy," Deseret Book Company, Salt Lake City, 1986, p 83

99 Nibley, *The Ancient State, "Paths That Stray," p 413*

100 Ibid., p 411

101 Warren Weaver, "The Imperfections of Science," *American Scientist* 49 (March 1961): 100 (quoted by Nibley, *The Ancient State*, p 411)

102 P.B. Medawar, "Is the Scientific Paper Fraudulent?" *Journal of Human Relations* 13 (1965): 6. (Quoted by Nibley, *The Ancient State*, p 411)

103 Ibid., 5 (411)

104 Albert Einstein, quoted in James T. Adams e al., *Living Philosophies,* (New York: Simon and Schuster, 1931), 6 (Quoted from Nibley, *The Ancient State*, p 411

105 *Science Daily;* www.sciencedaily.com/terms/placebo_effect.htm

106 "The Power of the Placebo Effect," Harvard Men's Health Watch, Harvard Health Publishing; https://www.health.harvard.edu/mental-health/the-power-of-the-placebo-effect

107 Gandhi, *The Way to God*, p 69

108 *The New Testament,* Hebrews 11:1

109 Gandhi, *The Way to God*, p 45

110 *The Book of Mormon*, Alma 32:21

111 David Gatten, *personal communication*

112 Neil L. Anderson, "Faith is not by Chance, but by Choice," General Conference talk, Nov, 2015

113 *The New Testament,* Mark 9:23

114 Louis Fischer, *The Life of Mahatma Gandhi,* The Easton Press, Norwalk, Connecticut, 1988, p 89

115 Ralph Waldo Emerson, "Self Reliance," p 35

116 William George Jordan, *The Power of Truth,* The Deseret Book Co. 1952, p 21

117 William George Jordan, *The Power of Truth*, p. 18

118 Dale Carnegie, *How to Win Friends and Influence People*; Simon & Schuster, New York, 1964

119 Jordan, p 106

120 *Doctrine & Covenants,* Section 93:40

121 Ned Miller, songwriter, "Do What You Do Do Well," Capitol Records 1965

122 *The Book of Mormon*, Moroni 10:4-5

123 *The Pearl of Great Price,* Moses 1:39

124 Ralph Waldo Emerson, "Spiritual Laws," p. 82

125 (D&C 101:16, Psalms 46:10)

126 Quote attributed to Henry Wadsworth Longfellow

127 *Doctrine & Covenants,* Section 93:1,28

INDEX

Thomas M. Carter, MD is a retired Family Practice/Emergency Medicine physician of 37 years of practice. Born in Bozeman, Montana, the son of Mark J. and Beth N. Carter, he was raised on a cattle ranch with 10 brothers and sisters in Montana, then in Ten Sleep, Wyoming at the foot of the Big Horn mountains. He attended Brigham Young University, Provo, Utah, and Creighton University School of Medicine. He completed his medical training at Naval Hospital, Camp Pendleton, CA.

Tom and his wife, Cindy are the parents of seven children and 17 (to date) grandchildren. Tom now lives in Evans, GA, and enjoys reading, writing, gardening, and time with his family and friends.

Also by Thomas M. Carter:

Badger, *What He Died For: In Memory of SEAL Mark T. Carter, SOC, USN,* 2017, Dorrance Publishing Co.
   ISBN: 978-1-4809-4158-8
   eISBN: 978-1-4809-4181-6